Pursuit

Pursuit

TOWARDS DEEPER INTIMACY WITH GOD

Ruth Conlon

Illustrations by Sylvi Conlon

EternalLife

EternalLife ◆
Investing in Eternity one word at a time

EternalLife Publishers is a publishing ministry with a passion for spiritual development. We produce individual and group resources to accompany you on your sacred journey. For more information on the training and products we provide go to www.eternallifepublishers.com.

Published by EternalLife Publishers
London, England
www.eternallifepublishers.com

Book Layout ©2013 BookDesignTemplates.com
Sylvia Conlon created all illustrations in this book.
Cover designed by EternalLife Publishers

Pursuit / Ruth Conlon. —1st ed.
ISBN   978-0-9934696-0-2

Contents

To

My Mum and Dad
For being God's hands on earth,
In the worst time in my life,
For truly being stars in the night season
And paying the price
For me to be here today, I love you.

To

Karen, what a friend, sister, confidant,
Always there, showing me the true meaning of loyalty and
commitment
Thank you for holding me up,
Wiping my tears and
Making such and impact in my life,
I'm forever grateful.

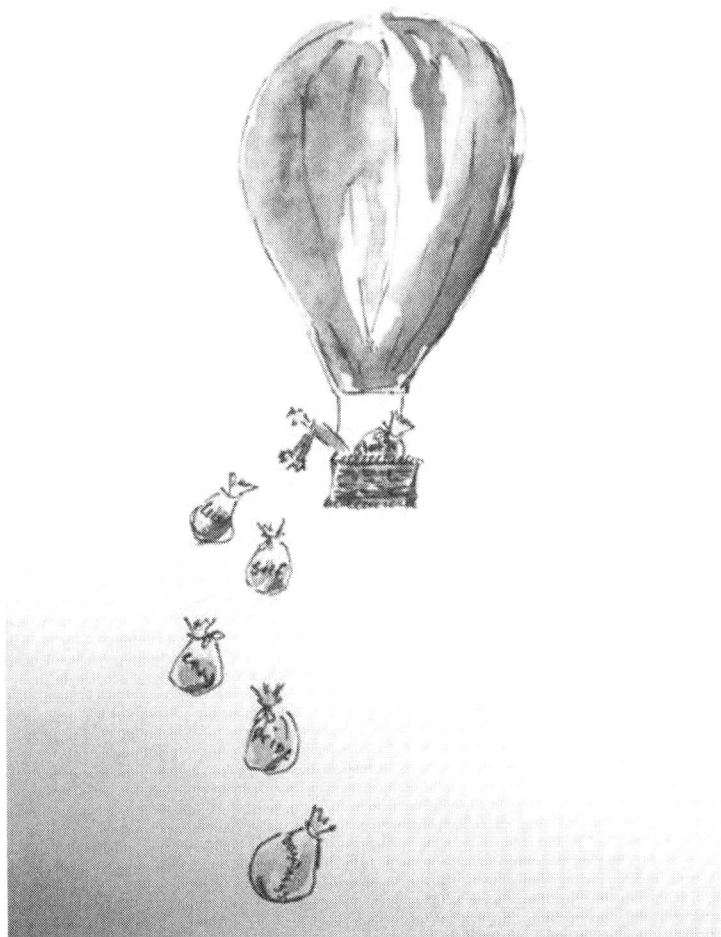

"Millions call themselves by His name, it is true, and pay some token homage to Him, but a simple test will show how little He is really honored among them. Let the average man be put to the proof on the question of who or what is ABOVE, and his true position will be exposed. Let him be forced into making a choice between God and money, between God and men, between God and personal ambition, God and self, God and human love, and God will take second place every time. Those other things will be exalted above. However the man may protest, the proof is in the choice he makes day after day throughout his life."

— A W Tozer – The Pursuit of God

Preface

I must admit, I have a bee in my bonnet. Those closest to me will tell you that after just a short time and when I feel comfortable, it's very easy for me to share it. So I thought it would be a good idea to relate to you at the beginning of the book my passion, my prayer, and my burden. I would love for many to join me in prayer about the current epidemic in modern day church.

When we look at our Western culture, the state of the church, and the souls of those who claim to be making it to heaven, we see worldly, carnal people content with our condition, with no desire or longing for holiness. We do not have the evident progression into Christlikeness that is required as we grow from glory to glory.

The Bible tells a story of five virgins carrying their lamps, which represent the Word of God and celebrating the coming of our Saviour. No, let me get that right—they are actually celebrating being saved from their sins since they cannot be waiting for someone they do not know or do not care to invest their time in knowing. Yet because of their lack of investment in the things of the Spirit and in developing a relationship with Christ, they have no oil and are in the end excluded from the kingdom of God.

This story brings me to tears, not only in writing this but also in my prayers. Sadly, it is a story that is very evident all around us as we have a generation who simply do not know God yet are supposedly leading the sheep to salvation. Instead they are actually being led to the slaughter, as they are ill informed of the way home and ill equipped to find it. When, by God's grace, they are informed, they find a strong opposition and resistance from their own hardened hearts, as they desire the things of the world. Their unwillingness to count the cost or pay the price by giving up their toys and taking up their crosses leaves them void of an authentic relationship with Christ. They have eyes but cannot see and ears but cannot hear. People who bear the truth have become so rare that they are classified as being mad, heretics, or simply bewitched. They continue in their burden to pull the elect out of the fire of the secularisation of the church and to be truly sanctified and separated unto God. But who will come and truly serve God? It hardly looks attractive to the carnal mind in comparison to the fashionable, worldly alternative that is void of suffering through bearing one's cross. The world promotes self, pride, pleasure, and independence of God the Holy Spirit.

Oh, that God would show us the emptiness and vanity of this present world! We still have eternity to come face-to-face with God's judgment—judgment that will bring into account every secret thing we have done. How can we be so deceived, so lost, and so focused on our short time here on earth? My desire is for us to live this life in a way that we invest in eternity. Like athletes, our time here on earth is to train for the everlasting crown and medal. We need to get to know and love Jesus while we have time, while we begin to hate sin and all that takes us away from Him. My prayer is that we live every day with the Day of Judgment in our mind's eye, so that we are prepared to give account of the way we have conducted ourselves. This is not a game, not a joke. This is the time we have been given to ensure we build our relationship with Jesus and are transformed into His image until He is fully formed in us. Many believe it is impossible, but they haven't attempted to yield themselves to the Holy Spirit for Him to do His work. The Bible says those who strive will enter in, yet they strive not, so they enter not. My prayer is that this book will ignite a serious examination of our lives in light of Scripture so that when He returns, we will not be found wanting.

"There is within the human heart a tough fibrous root of fallen life whose nature is to possess, always to possess. It covets 'things' with a deep and fierce passion. The pronouns 'my' and 'mine' look innocent enough in print, but their constant and universal use is significant. They express the real nature of the old Adamic man better than a thousand volumes of theology could do. They are verbal symptoms of our deep disease. The roots of our hearts have grown down into things, and we dare not pull up one rootlet lest we die. Things have become necessary to us, a development never originally intended. God's gifts now take the place of God, and the whole course of nature is upset by the monstrous substitution."

A. W. Tozer, The Pursuit of God

Introduction

This book is based on six years of experience of encountering God. It is a direct response to my prayer, "Break me down until there is nothing left but You." I decided that if, in the end, it's just going to be God and His Word that stands, then I wanted to be prepared and on the right side of the cross before that happened—not building up things in this world that didn't count and would be burnt as unprofitable work. At the time of my prayer, I had too much keeping me busy and away from His presence. I was a hypocrite, saying I loved God while living for myself. My daily twenty-four hours were filled with everything but Him.

I had a form of godliness, but God was not Lord over my life. I claimed to love God, yet I was not totally abandoned to Him. I would soon learn that none of the things I preoccupied myself with mattered, as each piece of my life was stripped away from me bit by bit—my marriage, my home, my business, my reputation, and me. My prayer was answered. I lost a lot, but I gained everything and learned a great deal along the way.

Pursuit of a deeper intimacy with God will be both the race of your life and the fight of your life. I want to encourage you to put on your seatbelt and hold on tight. Things will get rough, and you will encounter obstacles and strong opposition as you pursue a deeper intimacy with God. There will be times when you will want to throw in the towel. You will believe you've messed up too badly or don't have the strength to go on. There will be times when the Enemy of your soul will say, "Why bother? Life was a lot easier without seeking God." But you must determine in your heart: "I am going to pursue the heart of God, and nothing is going to stop me. If I fall down, I must get back up." God knows your weaknesses. He knows who you are, and His arms are ever open to receive you. Regardless of what the devil tries to tell you, brace yourself and don't let go of God. Remember, a righteous man falls seven times and gets right back up

(Prov. 24:14). When you fall, run into His arms. He will forgive you and resume your pursuit without delay.

There are times in my walk when I would just sit down and say to myself, "This is hard!" Sometimes I see struggles and battles against my soul that seem to have no end in sight, despite my frequent prayers. I look at God's will and then at my life, and there is a big gulf in between. My strong desire for God, together with God cheering me on—even after my greatest falls—gets me back on my feet. I've learned the hard way that the deeper we get into God's presence, the fiercer the battle. But this is just evidence that we're doing the right thing and going in the right direction. The Devil wants us to give up and live a carnal life, thereby forfeiting all God has for us in His kingdom.

One vital truth I've learned is that when we fall or a besetting sin keeps recurring, instead of running for cover and hiding like Adam and Eve, we must become aware of our inability to change any habits in our lives. God is teaching us humility and total dependency on Him. Without God, we can truly do nothing (John 15:5). Paul rejoiced in his weakness because when we are weak, God is strong (2 Cor. 12:10). Only when we give our weakness and our mess over to Him will He sort it out. He will take our burden. Just like the old hymn used to say:

What a friend we have in Jesus,
All our sins and grief to bear!
What a privilege to carry
Everything to God in prayer!
O what peace we often forfeit,
O what needless pain we bear,
All because we do not carry
Everything to God in prayer.

Have we trials and temptations?
Is there trouble anywhere?
We should never be discouraged;
Take it to the Lord in prayer.
Can we find a friend so faithful?
Who will all our sorrows share?
Jesus knows our every weakness;
Take it to the Lord in prayer.

Are we weak and heavy laden?
Cumbered with a load of care?
Precious Savior, still our refuge;
Take it to the Lord in prayer.
Do thy friends despise, forsake thee?
Take it to the Lord in prayer!
In his arms he'll take and shield thee;
Thou wilt find a solace there.[1]

---

[1] Joseph M. Scriven, "What a Friend We Have in Jesus," 1855

The Truth about Grace

One of the deceptions God opened my eyes to is the phenomenon term described as *cheap grace.*

> *"Cheap grace is the grace we bestow on ourselves. Cheap grace is the preaching of forgiveness without requiring repentance, baptism without church discipline, Communion without confession.... Cheap grace is grace without discipleship, grace without the cross, grace without Jesus Christ, living and incarnate."* *"Of course you have sinned, but now everything is forgiven, so you can stay as you are and enjoy the consolations of forgiveness."* *The main defect of such a proclamation is that it contains no demand for discipleship. In contrast to this is costly grace: "costly grace confronts us as a gracious call to follow Jesus, it comes as a word of forgiveness to the broken spirit and the contrite heart. It is costly because it compels a man to submit to the yoke of Christ and follow him; it is grace because Jesus says: "My yoke is easy and my burden is light."*[2]

Dietrich Bonhoeffer explains this so well, and today, more than ever, we have a generation of professing Christians who believe they can come as they are and stay as they are with no progression into the things of God. Modern-day Christianity has deceived many into believing that saying a prayer one time in our lives entitles us to heaven, even though we live like the world seven days a week. This is a lie because the Word tells

---

[2] http://www.scrollpublishing.com/store/Bonhoeffer.html.

us to take off the old man and put on Christ. Nevertheless, modern Christians no longer do this. There is no more pressing into the things of God. The scary thing is that professing Christians are not living according to the instructions given in God's Word and are so blinded by deception that, even when they hear the truth, they take no action to seek God to change their lives so they will be able to walk according to His plan.

Unwittingly, many progressing saints are heading to eternal damnation, as they make no effort to sow seeds on earth to invest in eternity. I believe it is important that I share this in the introduction because many people will believe they are saved and need not pursue God or that they can live their lives just as they please with no consequences. We must remember that baptism means our old lives die as we go down into the water, and as we come up, it is no longer us who lives but Christ. If we decide to take our lives back and live them our way, we also take back the consequences.

Obedience

Many people believe that being a Christian is about having information and knowing things about God.

But no one gets to heaven by simply knowing of Him. The Bible says that even the demons know Him (James 2:19). It is important that before we dive into the text of this book, we discuss the necessity in our Christian walk to be fully surrendered and committed to Jesus, which is expressed in our obedience to His Word.

"He who has My commandments and keeps them, it is he who loves Me. And he who loves Me will be loved by My Father, and I will love him and manifest Myself to him." Judas (not Iscariot) said to Him, "Lord, how is it that You will manifest Yourself to us, and not to the world?" Jesus answered and said to him, "If anyone loves Me, he will keep My word; and My Father will love him, and We will come to him and make Our home with him. He who does not love Me does not keep My words; and the word which you hear is not Mine but the Father who sent Me." (John 14:21–24 NKJV)

From the above Scripture, we can see that if we love God, we will keep His commandments. This, in reverse, means that if we do not keep His commandments, we cannot claim to love Him or even be connected to Him. Loving God and keeping His Word and His ways are clear indications of whether we are His children or whether we are simply playing church.

We must also realise that we are accountable for what we know. On judgment day, we will have to give account for the things we heard and did not implement in our lives. James 1:21–26 says the following:

"Therefore lay aside all filthiness and overflow of wickedness, and receive with meekness the implanted word, which is able to save your souls. But be doers of the word, and not hearers only, deceiving yourselves. For if anyone is a hearer of the word and not a doer, he is like a man observing his natural face in a mirror; for he observes himself, goes away, and immediately forgets what kind of man he was. But he who looks into the perfect law of liberty and continues in it, and is not a forgetful hearer but a doer of the word, this one will be blessed in what he does." (NKJV)

Many people gather information through books, conferences, and Sunday services and never make any advancement in their spiritual growth. The bottom line is that it is not what we know that is important but what we do. In modern Christianity we can see that this *doing* of God's commands has labelled those who attempt to live it out as being legalistic. There is widespread confusion about the real definition of legalism, and we hear statements like, "The law of God is no longer relevant as we are under grace," or "He's taking his walk too seriously. He is just legalistic." These are some of the misconceptions people associate with those who attempt to live in accordance with God's Word.

Many things that will be covered in this book will challenge and cause people to re-evaluate whether they are building their houses on sand or on a rock and whether it will stand the test of time. It will challenge delusions and values that have been held for decades. Unless we build solid foundations, our houses will be destroyed when the storm comes. Surrendering and making a commitment to God means being willing to listen to God's Word and living in obedience to it.

Legalism

The funny thing is that many Christians have started to define obedience as legalism because of the lack of knowledge concerning the biblical requirement of obedience to God's Word. Often people who attempt to live in obedience to the Word of God in every detail of their lives are seen to be taking their walk a bit too seriously. If they have resolved to live their lives in prayer, holiness, and developing themselves in line with Scripture, they are likely to be ridiculed not only by non-Christians but also those who are professing Christians.

Further still, there is a common delusion that the New Testament has erased obedience to the Word and that grace covers us. This has caused many to be careless about their Christian walk, and unwittingly they have walked right out of the narrow way and onto the broad way alongside the many who do not *do* the words of Christ and will not enter heaven (Matt. 7:21–23). It is not that this 'doing' justifies a person—far from it! But this doing is birthed out of love and is a response to the justification we have received from God by faith. We see several Scriptures in the Bible that bring us right back to God's requirement for obedience. The true definition of legalism is someone who is using his or her works of following the law as justification to gain salvation.

Obedience isn't doing with the intention that this doing will gain our salvation, something we can only receive from God by faith, not through works. The obedience we are talking about is birthed out of a response to justification, an act of love and devotion, and a deep desire to love God and please God in everything. It is not done to gain heaven but because God has saved us! We respond to Him through obedience, which His Word says is proof we truly love Him.

The error in the definition of legalism has caused many Christians to refrain from being obedient or to develop spiritually so as not to be seen as legalists. Others still intellectualise it by saying, "I must look into this in more detail." They say this as a form of avoidance to deviate from their responsibility and call to obedience.

I pray that as you read this book, God will open your eyes and your spirit and will speak to your heart as you accept His invitation to go deeper.

CHAPTER ONE

Ancient Paths

Pursuing the Heart of God

As we look throughout the Bible and through the course of church history, we find ancient paths and trails of individuals who were in hot pursuit for the heart of God. This pursuit was not about learning or acquiring knowledge about God from the Bible or even about having an understanding of the church and gaining spiritual insights. It was about something a lot deeper; it was about them having a close and intimate relationship with God, where they truly knew Him on a personal level.

We have people just like David in the Bible, who wrote love songs and psalms to God and was described "as a man after God's own heart" (Acts 13:22). You can see by David's writing that he did not merely know of God (knowledge and information), but he knew Him experientially. Through David's writing, you can see his relentless pursuit of God's presence. Psalm 27:4 says, "One thing I have desired of the Lord, that will I seek: That I may dwell in the house of the Lord all the days of my life, to behold the beauty of the Lord, and to inquire in His temple." David was so in love with God that he had a desire to build a tabernacle unto God. Second Samuel 7:1–2 says, "Now it came to pass when the king was dwelling in his house, and the Lord had given him rest from all his enemies all around, that the king said to Nathan the prophet, 'See now, I dwell in a house of cedar, but the ark of God dwells inside tent curtains.'" But this relationship was mutual.

As we take a closer look, we begin to see more examples of those who had an intimate relationship with God. One such person was Enoch. Although not much has been said in the Bible about Enoch, he walked with God and was faithful, despite being in the midst of a perverse and wicked generation. Genesis 5:

21–22, 24 says, "Enoch lived sixty-five years, and begot Methuselah. After he begot Methuselah, Enoch walked with God three hundred years, and had sons and daughters. … And Enoch walked with God; and he was not, for God took him" (NKJV). Looking further on, we see the relationship Jesus had with His disciples. They ate together and laughed together, and John, described as the beloved, even rested on Jesus' bosom. John 13:23 says, "Now there was leaning on Jesus' bosom one of His disciples, whom Jesus loved" (NKJV).

As we look into church history, we see people like the desert fathers and mothers—Christian monks who lived a life of fasting, prayer, solitude, and poverty during the early part of the third century. These Christians fled the cities to live in the Egyptian deserts in search of a life of simplicity devoted to God and unencumbered by worldly comforts. Their closeness to God, practice of righteousness, and wise advice is documented in Thomas Merton's *The Wisdom of the Desert*.[3] They were so in love with God that they abandoned all worldly comforts and offerings, seeking solitude with God in the desert. We see this same devotion in the lives of monks and nuns throughout history, including Saint Teresa of Avila, who wrote

---

[3] Thomas Merton, *The Wisdom of the Desert* (New York: New Directions Book, 1970)

Interior Castle,[4] where she describes her soul's journey into intimacy with God.

We have so many examples of people who were in hot pursuit of God and in turn impacted their generation, like William Law, John Wesley, Charles Spurgeon, Leonard Ravenhill, and A. W. Tozer and women like Mother Teresa, Madame Guyon, and Corrie Ten Boom, just to mention a few. Now God is inviting us to come away with Him into a deeper relationship. Will you come?

In my own search for the heart of God, I have followed the paths of nuns, desert fathers, Baptists, Methodists, Anglicans, and Pentecostals. All had an earnest passion for God and pursued Him and Him alone with total abandonment. They lived their lives focused on the one thing, as Mary, Anna, and David exemplified.

In Psalm 27:4, we can clearly see that David was in pursuit of God. The one thing he desired was to dwell in God's presence. David pursued intimacy with God. This can be seen through his writings in Psalms. This was his desire. God was his passion—the one he thirsted after (Ps. 42).

In the same manner, we look at the life of Mary in Luke 10:38–42, which says:

---

[4] Teresa of Avila, *Interior Castle: The Soul's Spiritual Journey to Union with God* (Florida: Bridge-Logos, 2008).

"Now it happened as they went that He entered a certain village; and a certain woman named Martha welcomed Him into her house. And she had a sister called Mary, who also sat at Jesus' feet and heard His word. But Martha was distracted with much serving, and she approached Him and said, 'Lord, do You not care that my sister has left me to serve alone? Therefore tell her to help me.' And Jesus answered and said to her,

> *"Martha, Martha, you are worried and troubled about many things. But one thing is needed, and Mary has chosen that good part, which will not be taken away from her." (NKJV)*

The one thing that was required Mary fulfilled by sitting at Jesus' feet, listening, developing intimacy with Jesus, and spending quality time with Him. Anna, a prophetess in the New Testament, was described as giving herself to prayer and fasting, while continually living in the temple. These three people show how they searched and lived for that one thing that was important. David did so by seeking and yearning, Mary by setting her focus solely on Christ, dwelling in His presence, and listening, and Anna by giving herself totally to prayer and fasting.

Jesus wasn't just a Sunday form of recreation or a social membership with duties. To them, Jesus was everything; He invaded their lives 24–7 as they

made way for Him in total surrender and abandonment, holding back nothing.

This level of commitment absolutely excites
me as I believe the almighty God, the creator of heav-
en and earth, deserves nothing less than our total surrender. Jesus didn't ask for a part of our lives, but
would we be willing to give everything? Would we be
willing to give even our very own lives? This is truly
the race of your life because it will cost you everything,
but we thank God we get in return Jesus living in and
through us as we walk as one.

This book is a testimony of the lessons I've
learned through my journey in pursuit of a greater intimacy with God away from the compromise and me-
diocrity of the modern-day church and into a personal,
loving, day-by-day walk with my Saviour. God knows
that along the way there have been some serious battles as the world tried to draw me in the opposite direction—and still does. My flesh forces me to fall to
things I have yet to train myself in. However, through
it all, I have God loving me, comforting me, wooing
me, and encouraging me. He is my greatest cheerlead-
er, saying, "You can make it! Just get back up and depend on Me."

I came to realise that falling is such a blessing
because we learn so much that enables us to stand and
walk longer. As we go into this journey, my prayer is

that you will encounter God. He's in love with you and desires every part of your life, every second of your day. He wants you to live conscious of His Spirit and responsive to His call by desiring the things that keep the relationship alive.

My sister and I were brought up by my great aunt who was passionate about Christ. In our house, we didn't just worship God on Sunday, as is so prevalent in Christianity today. It was a lifestyle of seeking and getting closer to God daily. I thank God for all the lessons learnt in my childhood that have become invaluable spiritual foundations, which have made my pursuit not seem so foreign.

Nevertheless, as God used the storms of life to break me down and humble me, the church became more and more lacking for me. I was not experiencing the same sense of God's power in the local church as I did as a child. I felt it was Christless and empty. The prayer meetings had disappeared, being replaced with concerts, and the church I had grown to love no longer existed.

The sad thing about it was that everyone else seemed fine with it. They seemed to have not known anything better and were satisfied with church as usual. Coffee mornings, toddler groups, women's meetings, and workers' meetings were all present, but no Christ, no personal transformation, and no presence of His glory. What really dampened my passion for Sunday worship was the fear that if Christ did walk into the service, He wouldn't be recognised.

I realised that the fundamental truth about Christianity had left the pulpits. People were no longer preparing for eternity, singing, "Good-bye, world." In fact, they believed just saying yes to God at one point of their lives with no daily seeking the kingdom of God was all they needed to prepare for the coming kingdom. In fact, the modern-day church didn't decrease in numbers since we could now come in, sit down, and never be challenged about our sin and the way we lived. This brought tears to my eyes. Hell was never spoken about. There were clearly parts of Scripture that you could tell, for years, had never got a look in.

My heart was breaking. I couldn't understand why we were sleeping. I got so frustrated. I just didn't know what I could do to show people that there was more than that. God requires us to get up higher and to have a relationship with Him, not a social gathering to emotionally stir people up for a few minutes and then mingle with their friends afterward. This walk is not about us. It's about Him. Yes, fellowship is essential but not a replacement for seeking God. We have been taught a Christianity where we create another Christ and delude ourselves that we are following His will—dissatisfied and discontent, with no change in character, looking more worldly than Christlike, and actually not caring for the truth. This has all been prophesied. In the last days, people will be lovers of themselves and not God (2 Tim. 3:2).

This is the time we live in—the last days—and we have to really work out our salvation with fear and trembling (Phil. 2:12). Many in the body who were once on fire for God have fallen asleep. The Bible says,

> *"Watch therefore, for you do not know what hour your Lord is coming" (Matt. 24:42).*

The scary thing is that the people who are spiritually sleeping actually think they are awake and that they can see. What a deception! Lord, wake us up; open our ears and eyes again. Wake up our brothers and sisters. We have become blind because of our constant disobedience to God's Word, our compromise, and our unwillingness to change. God will instruct and guide us; He has given us His Word. But when we decide we don't want to change, there are consequences. Second Thessalonians 2:11–12 states, "And for this reason God will send them strong delusion, that they should believe the lie, that they all may be condemned who did not believe the truth but had pleasure in unrighteousness" (NKJV).

We have fallen in love with the world, and unlike the saints of old, we are creating our own heaven now. We spend thirty minutes of our day—if that—to invest in our eternal destination. Then we live like the world the rest of the time. We even have good intentions to get closer to God. These are, however, clouded by our other worldly commitments that have become a greater priority to us than our walk with God and our heavenly (eternal) destination.

Many people will be shocked in the end because the Bible says whatever we sow we will reap. Galatians 6:8 states, "For he who sows to his flesh will of the flesh reap corruption, but he who sows to the Spirit will of the Spirit reap everlasting life." We can't live like the world and expect to actually have a heavenly destination. Where has this deception come from? Even Paul said he had to keep his flesh under control so he did not lose that which he had attained (1 Cor. 9:7). Why should we be different? People shouldn't be shocked or fooled since we see the evidence of sowing and reaping on a daily basis. Athletes, doctors, and even school children spend years of their lives studying and preparing. Why do we suppose we don't need more than thirty minutes a day to prepare for eternity?

Like everything else, we decided we would make the grace of God fit our carnal agendas. "Christ died for my sins. I'm free by grace. I'm saved by grace.

I don't have to do anything myself." What a mistake—an error that will see many professing Christians refused entry into heaven. The Word of God clearly says that faith without works is dead. It's only by God's grace and mercy that the door of salvation is opened to us.

Nevertheless, we see instructions in the Bible telling us to fight, press on, practice, take off, put on, and run. These are all active words, calling us to action. Yes, Christ has done it, but we now have to act to obtain that which has been given to us freely.

If we received a letter from a lawyer saying our long-lost aunty had left an inheritance for us, we would tell all our friends. However, unless we take the necessary steps to obtain the inheritance, we will be no better off than before.

This is the case with our spiritual progression into the fullness of God. God has promised in His Word that we will be like Christ. His Word talks about us coming into the full stature of Christ. This means as we progress in this world, there is more of Him in us, and this is what we pursue. However, in this pursuit, we see areas in our lives that don't line up. We go back to God in earnest prayer (because our lives depend on it). As we resist the devil, through the power of the Holy Spirit released in prayer, he flees, and we get the victory.

When we seek God's will for our lives and want to progress spiritually, we will sometimes want to change negative habits in our own strength, trying to free ourselves. This is actually a total waste of time and energy and can be very frustrating to say the least. "It's not by might or by power but by His Spirit, says the Lord" (Zech. 4:6). We are simply required to analyse our lives in light of Christ and Scripture, to pray, and fast earnestly for change. God then, through the Holy Spirit, gives us the power, the grace, and the anointing to overcome each hurdle and every besetting sin.

God was waiting for me to come to the end of myself and to the end of my strength. Once I knew I could do nothing of myself, I cried to God and asked Him to deliver me, and God is so faithful. Resisting became so easy because it was no longer me but the Holy Spirit enabling me. The Bible says in Matthew 11:28–30, "Come to Me, all *you* who labour and are heavy laden, and I will give you rest. Take My yoke upon you and learn from Me, for I am gentle and lowly in heart, and you will find rest for your souls. For My yoke *is* easy and My burden is light" (NKJV). I started to have a living encounter of this through the hard experience of letting go and depending on God to set me free from the sins that kept me bound. Now when He reveals an area in my life that needs refining, I seek Him with tears and prayer, knowing it is only through His power that I can truly see change. Every time He makes it easier, anointing me and lifting me above addictions and sins that used to control me.

Totally Abandoned

God created us with a desire to be totally abandoned to Him. In fact, this is the greatest thirst of the human soul that can only be quenched when our heart is fully devoted to God. Matthew 22:35–38 says, "Then one of them, a lawyer, asked *Him a question,* testing Him, and saying, 'Teacher, which *is* the great commandment in the law?' Jesus said to him, "'you shall love the Lord your God with all your heart, with all your soul, and with all your mind.' This is *the* first and great commandment" (NKJV). God wants us to be fully devoted to Him in love so that we are completely His in everything. It is only through the Holy Spirit that He can change our hearts, so we can live in holiness in every aspect of our lives.

Pursuing God by Giving All

God is so in love with us, and He loves us with everything. In return, He wants us to respond by loving Him with our all. Just as we do in relationships, if we love someone deep inside, no matter how we try to hide it, we also want him or her to love us. Sometimes we desire the same love, but sometimes we want even more.

Many of us may even struggle with thinking this is a big ask: "How can I love God with all my heart, soul, mind, and strength?" But this isn't done by our effort. This, like everything else we receive in the kingdom, is a gift from God given to us through the Holy Spirit. God Himself will pour into us that love to desire and love Him in the way that He requires. Romans 5:5 says: **"Now hope does not disappoint, because the love of God has been poured out in our hearts by the Holy Spirit who was given to us"** (NKJV).

This love that is poured out by the Holy Spirit must be done like everything else, in humility and heartfelt prayer—with the acknowledgment and realisation that without God we are spiritually poor in spirit unless He gives us the things we require to delve deeper in the ways of the spirit. We cannot be an inactive part of this process, but if we see that our hearts lack a deep love for God, we must pray, "Lord, with You all things are possible. Please forgive me for any way I have hindered Your progress in my life. I pray that You will pour out Your love into my heart and increase my capacity to love You." As we pray this prayer in earnest, the Holy Spirit will increase our capacity to love Him and to go deeper.

Pursuing God by Loving Others

Part of our human nature is the longing to be loved. This is the way we were created. God also has this same desire to be loved. The more we love Jesus and fall in love with God, the more the natural progression will occur that we will be able to fulfil the second commandment: "And *the* second *is* like it: 'You shall love your neighbour as yourself'" (Matt. 22:39 NKJV).

This is why many people within the church complain that they feel like there is a lack of love. If someone was really going through a storm, where would he or she run to? There is no longer the sincere concern around the broken stranger or for the people who walk through the door. It's just church as usual. We greet our friends and show partiality. The broken couldn't even come in because our hearts have become so self-orientated that, even if they did, we might not recognise them. From my own experience, I can say that it is possible to worship with believers in the morning and contemplate suicide on the same day without anybody's knowledge. How very heartbreaking and sad. This is why people on the streets, even our youth, are engaging with drug dealers and criminals. We seem to have lost our compassion for those on the outside in favour of our Christian friends on the inside.

When we do decide to say hello to someone in church, often it isn't from our hearts. It is simply birthed from our Christian duty or even worse, to be recognised and applauded for being such a lovely respectable person. Yet God checks our hearts and checks our motives. "Oh, what a giver! She always makes everyone feel welcome," someone may say. But when the same person you said hello to can't make it to church, who goes to find that lost sheep? When the service is over, who continues to love, not out of duty but because of the sincere, deep-rooted love that is flowing out of one's heart to touch another? This is merely a reflection of our hearts towards God. "[20] If someone says, 'I love God,' and hates his brother, he is a liar; for he who does not love his brother whom he has seen, how can he love God whom he has not seen?" (1 John 4:20 NKJV).

We truly examine our hearts using the measure with which we love the broken and the stranger and how much compassion or concern we have. How much love and support do we show others in secret when no one else is watching? How do we treat the stranger or the poor when they enter our midst? These are the questions we need to ask ourselves as fellow believers, not making excuses for having no contact with broken people. We just have to walk to the job centre or the local courtroom to see thousands of people looking for someone to catch them with the love of God. They just don't know it yet.

Some of our gatherings have become so prestigious that the broken and the poor couldn't afford to get in, let alone sit down. We have created our places of fellowship to be the meeting places of the rich and shameless while we praise ourselves for doing things we should be doing as a matter of course. We really need to get back to the heart of things, of loving God and truly loving our neighbour. We have to seek God earnestly for a heart transformed by His Word. He promised, "I will put My laws in their mind and write them on their hearts; and I will be their God, and they shall be My people" (Heb. 8:10 NKJV). Oh that this would be our reality.

As we progress in this chapter, we will see that it is not possible to love people genuinely if we don't first get connected with God. This connection must be one of love and intimacy, and as it grows and develops, loving others will be natural and effortless. It will simply overflow from the love we have from God. It is so important that this first commandment takes precedence in every area of our lives. It must be our first priority. We need to return to our first love. This love relationship with God must be first, not putting it to the side for other so-called demanding issues that are of no eternal value.

Pursuing God by Drawing Near

God's Word says, "Draw near to God and He will draw near to you" (James 4:8 NKJV). What a wonderful invitation. We must have a *selah* moment, pause to understand the full power and extent of what is being said in James 4:8. The maker of heaven and earth is inviting us to draw near to Him. Think about it. What a lovely God! Many people suffer from loneliness and rejection, but God has a track record through the Bible of loving everyone, despite His people turning their backs on Him. He has had His fair share of rejection and loneliness. It is worse still when the object of His affection doesn't love Him back and gives Him a half-hearted response. Real love, even in the human sense, is full of passion. Everything is yearning, the butterflies in the stomach, and waiting by the phone. It is as if all the cells in our bodies are waiting in expectation for the one we love. I don't know if you have ever waited for someone you love, but if you have, you'll understand what I am talking about.

I remember when I was about eighteen (young, foolish, really naïve, and full of the world). It was Valentine's Day, and I spent the day buying stuff and cooking and doing my best to look great. I was supposed to meet my companion at 7:00 p.m. Finally, everything was ready, and I was so excited. Seven o'clock came and went, and he didn't show. I went to the window, looked at my phone, nothing. Eight o'clock came and went as well, and again I went to the window, opened the front door, and even called his phone. Again, nothing. By this point my heart had already sunk. I was feeling heartbroken and rejected. By the time nine o'clock came and went, I had changed and went to bed, only to find I couldn't sleep.

When we look at the story of the Prodigal Son (Luke 15:11–32), the father in the story saw his son from far off. The father must have been looking, waiting, and praying that his son would come home. That's love. It's passionate, yet when love is not reciprocated, boy can it hurt. When I finally saw the man I had prepared dinner for, his casual dismissal of the situation was even more painful than the pain I felt on Valentine's night.

We need to really come to grips with the fact that God loves *us*! The Bible is simply a love story of His pursuit for us. I pray that we don't cause God pain as He waits for our response to His love. I pray that we don't break His jealous (Ex. 34:14) heart and keep Him waiting in vain. I pray that we don't give our love for the Creator to created things and the things of the world, with their fleeting pleasures. So often that is exactly what we do, only to give God, who gives us everything, the scraps of our lives. I pray that when God knocks at the door of our hearts, we will open and let Him in. "Behold, I stand at the door and knock. If anyone hears My voice and opens the door, I will come in to him and dine with him, and he with Me" (Rev. 3:20 NKJV).

God has already expressed His love by sending Jesus to the cross to die for our sins. "For God so loved the world that He gave His only begotten Son" (John 3:16 NKJV). In response to God's love and desire for us, we must, out of our own free will, seek Him out to enter into a deeper relationship with Him. In James 4:8, God invites us to get closer to Him. Our intimacy with God is determined by us and how serious we are about pursuing Him. God wants to be part of every aspect of our lives, but as the perfect gentleman He is, He will not occupy our space unless we call and invite Him in.

Pursuing through Obedience

As we seek deeper intimacy with God, we have to develop a relationship by getting to know what God likes and what He hates. If you have a friend who behaves in a manner that makes you feel very uncomfortable, more likely than not, the friendship will come to an end—unless the friend changes his or her habits. This is very similar to what happens when we start to pursue God.

We must understand that we convey our love for God through our obedience to His Word and His commandments. We communicate our love to God when we start hating sin as God hates sin. If we love God, we will hate the sight of our sin. Then when we see sin or even the resemblance of sin in our lives, we will fall humbly at His feet and pray for His grace to remove it from our hearts. As we patiently ask and seek Him for a change, we will be transformed by the power of the Holy Spirit, God's agent of change.

The evidence of loving God is when we in turn love His commandments, love His ways, and pursue them in love. Jesus said to His disciples in John 14:21, "He who has my commandments and keeps them, it is he who loves me. And he who loves Me will be loved by My Father, and I will love him and manifest Myself to Him" (NKJV).

We cannot live our lives contrary to God's commandments and Word and say we love Him. It would be like an unfaithful spouse who is unwilling to give up the adultery but saying, "I love you." It is simply a contradiction. We cannot compromise the Word of God and then say, "But I love God in my heart." The love God requires from us is a love that does not merely show in word but in deed also—in the deep issues of the heart and the way we live our lives.

David is described in the Bible as a man after God's own heart. It says in Psalm 119:11, "Your word I have hidden in my heart, that I might not sin against You."(NKJV). David was so in love with God that he didn't want anything in his heart or conduct to offend God. This is the same way we must meditate on God's Word, commandments, and ways. In addition, we need to ask the Holy Spirit to help us and empower us to align our lives to God's Word and will so we don't worship God with our mouths while our hearts and our lives don't reflect that. "Therefore the Lord said: 'Inasmuch as these people draw near with their mouths and honor Me with their lips, but have removed their hearts far from Me, and their fear toward Me is taught by the commandment of men'." (Isa. 29:13 NKJV).

In this day and age, there is a love of God that is promoted that is a love of God without obedience—without the holy fear of God. These professing Christians lack some fundamental truths, like holiness and sanctification. Everyone knows that our walk is progressive. However, there are some who should be mature enough to help others, yet they are still restricted in their growth.

"For though by this time you ought to be teachers, you need *someone* to teach you again the first principles of the oracles of God; and you have come to need milk and not solid food. For everyone who partakes *only* of milk *is* unskilled in the word of righteousness, for he is a babe. But solid food belongs to those who are of full age, *that is,* those who by reason of use have their senses exercised to discern both good and evil." (Heb. 5:12–14 NKJV)

This has a negative effect, and we are unable to experience the power of the Holy Spirit against sin in our lives, for some don't want to change or grow up. We are happy living our lives according to our agenda, using God merely as a rubber stamp. Others are just simply so weary because the love of the world has consumed their hearts. There is truly not enough room for God, yet, everything else we deem a priority. Some honestly desire change and are struggling to alter their habits. As a result, they fall down in defeat. But once we come to the end of self and realise that of ourselves we can do nothing, then we tearfully seek our spiritual redemption, yielding to the Holy Spirit. It is the Holy Spirit who takes over and delivers us, bringing us all progressively onto the pathway of holiness. As each shackle of sin is overcome by the power of the Holy Spirit, we can all find ourselves truly liberated.

Pursuing God by Cleansing Our Hands and Purifying Our Hearts

In James 4:8 when God asked us to draw near to Him and then He will draw near to us, we find the continuation of the verse to read, "Cleanse your hands, you sinners; and purify your hearts, you double-minded" (NKJV).

Part of drawing close to God is "cleansing our hands," which means to change the things we are doing and align our actions to God's Word. We can no longer live in a manner that is customary to the world. We must live in a fashion that follows the principles of the kingdom of God. And it is not merely our outward actions, as J. C. Ryle, the Anglican bishop of Liverpool, said in his writing about holiness: "Of course I need not tell anyone who reads his Bible with attention, that a man may break God's law in his heart and thought, when there is not an overt and visible act of wickedness. Our Lord has settled that point beyond dispute in the Sermon on the Mount (Matthew 5:21–28)."[5] Even a poet of our own time has truly said, "A man may smile and smile, and be a villain."[6]

There are also sins of omission as well as sins of commission. But I think it is necessary in these times

---

[5] J. C. Ryle, *Holiness* (Chicago: Moody, 2010), 16.
[6] Ibid.

to remind my readers that a man may commit sin and be ignorant of it and fancy himself innocent when in actuality, he is guilty. I fail to see any scriptural evidence for the modern assertion that "sin is not sin to us until we discern it and are conscious of it."[7] On the contrary, in the fourth and fifth chapters of that unduly neglected book, Leviticus, and in the fifteenth of Numbers, I find that Israel distinctly taught that there were sins of ignorance that rendered people unclean and needed atonement (Lev. 4:1–35, 5:14–19; Num. 15:25–29). I also find our Lord teaching that "the servant who knew not his master's will and did it not" was not excused on account of his ignorance but was beaten or punished (Luke 12:48 NKJV). We will do well to remember, that when we use our own miserable, imperfect knowledge and consciousness to measure our sinfulness, we are on very dangerous ground. A deeper study of Leviticus might do us much good.

J. C. Ryle clearly explains that being unaware of our sin isn't an excuse that will exclude us from punishment. We as Christians have to become personally familiar with the Word of God, examining our own lives against God's Word prayerfully in order for the Holy Spirit to reveal areas that need our attention and need mortification by His Spirit.

---

[7] Ibid

We need to look closely at God's Word and check our lives against it. We must ignore the lies that tell us God's grace will cover any sin being committed, when His Word clearly says, "What shall we say then? Shall we continue in sin that grace may abound? Certainly not! How shall we who died to sin live any longer in it?" (Rom 6:1–2).

CHAPTER TWO

God's Priority

First Things First

As we have been discussing, God is yearning and longing for our hearts and love. This is why His first and most important commandment is about loving Him. How amazing that God wants us to want Him too—not out of coercion but as a natural desire in response to His love. The most important thing to God is that we love Him. This must be our own personal measure of where we estimate our growth spiritually, as well as where we are in other areas of our lives.

When we look at our lives and see the different ways God has revealed Himself, we see that it was all for love. Each time He made known His secrets or revealed Himself, it was because He wanted us to go deeper in love and to partake of His love. More than any work or ministry we can do for God, our hearts come first in importance to Him. Once He has our hearts, His work will flow out of our intimacy with Him.

We may read the Bible or a book or go to a Christian conference and really get inspired to press into holiness and go deeper in our walk with God. But the stress and the fatigue will still come, and we may not be able to continue. The only people who are able to continue in this journey are those who are in love with God. Love will make us do crazy things. When we want to throw in the towel, the love of God will give us the strength and energy to carry on. The love of God will take us where mere zeal and excitement cannot. It is true, only love makes the world go around. To begin with, our love for God will empower us by the Holy Spirit to make a difference within our communities. So when the pressure does come, the sweet love of God will ignite us and give us the strength we need to persevere.

What we need to understand is that loving God isn't an alternative choice. It is the only way—as Jesus commands. He allows us to make the decision whether to draw near or not. Today there are so many Christian charities, ministries, and initiatives with a heart for changing the plight of others. This is essential to our call as Christians. But we must acknowledge that this is our secondary call as Christians. Our first and utmost call is to love God.

When we love God this deeply, it moves Him and changes us and other people we may encounter. Loving God has eternal value because as we love Him, we are being drawn closer, knowing Him more intimately. There are so many things that move God's heart. When we fall short of God's best for our lives and seek forgiveness, this touches God's heart, as we are showing a desire to walk according to His commands. God wants us to love Him with our very being and everything we do or give. It is a joy to His heart when it comes from a place of love.

As we try to put God first and make Him a priority in our lives, we find that it is not an easy process. At times you'll fall down, as we all do. But as long as we get back up and are diligent to make a determined attempt to pursue the heart of God, then that is all that matters. This must be our overarching pursuit, even above the pursuit of a reputation and the possessions of this world.

Now we are going to look a bit deeper to see what it means to love God with all our hearts, minds, strength, and souls.

With All My Mind

When we start to look at how we express our love to God with our hearts, souls, minds, and strength, we need to look at how this can be done on a day-by-day basis. We are going to look at ways we can use our minds, which consist of our thoughts, memories, and thinking, to love God. God's Word says, "For those who live according to the flesh set their minds on the things of the flesh, but those *who live* according to the Spirit, the things of the Spirit" (Rom. 8:5).

One of the ways we can love God with our minds is by setting our minds on things of the spirit. "To set" means to keep fixed or to keep in place. We need to develop a habit of keeping our minds on the Word. This can be done by singing hymns and worship songs or fixing our thoughts by meditating on the wonderful natural beauty around us and the things God has created. Often God speaks to me through the everyday occurrences that happen in nature, Psalm 19:1–4 describes it beautifully:

> *The heavens declare the glory of God; And the firmament shows His handiwork. Day unto day utters speech, and night unto night reveals knowledge. There is no speech nor language where their voice is not heard. Their line has gone out through all the earth, and their words to the end of the world. (NKJV)*

We need to renew our minds from the negative tapes and mind-sets we have taken on from the world, the lust, the guilt, the anger, and the shame. And we must follow Paul's instructions in Philippians 4:8:

"Finally, brethren, whatever things are true, whatever things are noble, whatever things are just, whatever things are pure, whatever things are lovely, whatever things are of good report, if there is any virtue and if there is anything praiseworthy—meditate on these things." (NKJV)

In order to set our minds on the things of the Spirit, we also have to remove our minds from the things of the world. In this age of technology, we have so many things competing for our minds. We get so much information on the go—e-mails, Facebook, updates from Twitter, not to mention endless selling by text and e-mails. It is a wonder that any of us are able to pull back our minds from the constant bombardment of society. What make things worse are the images used to sell even the simplest of things. Take for example toothpaste.

Why does it need to be advertised with somebody who is scantily dressed?

In order to set our minds on the things of the Spirit, we have to make some serious decisions about the things in our lives that are being used to keep our minds carnal and grounded in the world.

If we could give up our Internet or mobile phones for a week, we would be so surprised at how much peace we are able to retrieve. In fact, in this place of stillness and peace, we are able to become very aware of the images being blasted at us and the effect they are having. A good strategy is to leave technology in the car or just turn off our technology when we get home. We will surely find that we have more peace and the ability to spend quality time with our family and with God.

If you're anything like me, then you have many books and Bibles in your iPad, which makes it so easy to study. Yet at the same time, the temptation that sometimes arises is, "Oh, I wonder what the weather is like tomorrow," or "Let me just check this." I have had to discipline myself (which is not easy) to either switch it off when I'm not working or only use it for study. Everyone will find out what works for him or her and how best he or she is led. But in the end, what is important is that we achieve our aim of creating a space where we can set our minds on God, His kingdom, and His ways.

This will also affect the things we watch on TV because what goes in must come out. It may come out in the way we speak, the way we conduct ourselves, or the decisions we make. Spending numerous hours in front of the TV, watching secular television, is a very subtle but effective way of being seduced into the culture of this world. The sad thing is that because of today's standards, on secular television there is a vast quantity of dialogue full of profanity, immoral suggestions, or anything else that is against godly living—greed, sex, lusts of all kinds, and encouragement to yield to all of the vices available.

Our children are now exposed to television that encourages lewd and immoral thinking. So the programmes shown on the screen—even films and programmes that look innocent—still promote adultery and deception and are in contradiction to our goal of loving godly characteristics. As I've weaned myself off of watching movies, I have begun to notice a difference in my spirit. Now I can see the dulling results it has on a person's spirit. Some of us, after watching TV, attempt to pray or study the Word, but instead fall asleep. Why do we find it so difficult to put our minds on godly things? Why do our spirits feel so heavy? We've already filled them with garbage. It's just like gorging ourselves on food and then attempting to run three miles. It will be difficult to say the least.

Loving God with all our minds means we need to focus, just like those who are training to win a race. They are very careful about the things they put in their bodies. They wake up early and train before work. Some get a personal coach or join a gym to help them achieve their goal, and they are dedicated, committed, and focused.

The Bible says in 1 Corinthians 9:24–25, "Do you not know that those who run in a race all run, but one receives the prize? Run in such a way that you may obtain it. And everyone who competes for the prize is temperate in all things. Now they do it to obtain a perishable crown, but we for an imperishable crown" (NKJV).

In the same way a runner is careful about what food he eats, we must be careful to protect our minds. This is achieved by protecting the gates that allow things to enter our minds. So we must protect the eye gate, ear gate, nose gate, touch gate, and taste gate so that nothing will hinder us from loving God with all our minds.

I used to be a film fanatic; I mean I would go to the cinema and watch movies back to back. Whenever I got low or under pressure, instead of running to God, I would put on a movie to relax my mind. As I started to go deeper in my pursuit of God and began to love God with everything, I started to watch movies and films *with* Jesus. Let me explain. When I would put on a movie or watch TV, I would do so with Christ in mind—like He was in the room with me. After doing this for a time, I decided to give up watching TV or movies altogether. As we start watching movies this way, our spirits are immediately conflicted the moment someone curses or someone does something ungodly. Watching films on TV with Jesus was really convicting.

I believe this is a good practice in general. If we live our lives with Jesus always in mind, we are in step with the Holy Spirit. Having a conscious awareness of the presence of God will reduce our yielding to the things of the world and the flesh. There are so many things we wouldn't do if our parents were with us all the time, let alone if Jesus is constantly around. The fact is that He is constantly around us, but because we do not consciously acknowledge it, we live in a manner that at times offends the Holy Spirit. In all we do, we need to determine if what we are letting into our thinking space glorifies God and shows love towards Him or if it is carnal and keeps us earth bound.

Those who are in training get up early. They rise early to train before they become distracted by getting to work or organising the children for school. They know that once everything starts, time will be stolen from them. I used to take an early morning drive so I could pray. I would park outside one of our local gyms and watch the people coming to the gym to train for an hour or two before the day really begins. Some would even come out dressed and ready to go to work after training.

The many books I have read of great women and men of faith also seem to exemplify this point. They got up before sunrise to seek God early before anyone else was awake. There were also those who spent all night in prayer seeking the face of God. I was challenged by the seriousness of the people who would consistently wake up early every morning to keep physically fit and also by the men and women of old who kept spiritually fit by making an effort to meet God early. We need to set a time and place where we can spend quality time praying and fellowshipping with God. This is essential to get our minds and spirits ready for the rest of the day, meditating and thinking on God's Word and ways.

The people exercising in the gym regularly eat with one thing in mind: how to train to keep their bodies in shape. Likewise, we must eat things spiritually that will help us develop our minds. We need to read godly books of men and women of faith who have gone before us. We must meditate on the Word and listen to the preaching of righteous ministers of God. Indeed, we need to fill our lives with worship and praise and everything else that will assist us in loving God with our entire minds.

You may read all this and think, *Wow! This is a challenge. There's so much to do. Where do I start?* Just like the runner needs a coach, we need a coach in the Holy Spirit. If we invite Him in to support us and guide us through the process, He will help us one step at a time. This is promised in God's Word, which states, "The Spirit of truth, has come, He will guide you into all truth; for He will not speak on His own authority, but whatever He hears He will speak; and He will tell you things to come" (John 16:13 NKJV).

We can also take a look at nature and see how things grow and progress. When we plant a flower, it doesn't just sprout suddenly. It takes time to see the leaves. Then after a while, we see the bud and eventually a flower. While it was growing in the dark, under the dirt, we didn't see the roots going down to get water to give it life. There is a lot of growth underneath before there is any sprouting above.

As we try to make progress in loving God with our minds, we must in the same way not give up. We must not beat ourselves up if we fall. Like any developing habit, falling just means we need to get back up. Yes, we will most likely fall again because falling produces good material that we can use tomorrow. When we fall, we begin to identify the gaps and the things that cause us to fall. This information is good for creating a strategy to prevent us from falling over the same thing again. We thank God that, as we start pursuing Him and loving Him with our minds, we are not alone. He is right beside us—just like natural fathers and mothers support their toddlers to help them walk. He lets go sometimes but always catches us just before we fall. At the same time, He is smiling, clapping, and cheering us on with joy over the two steps we attempted to make towards His heart.

The Word of God

One of the most important things we need to do as we seek to love and honour God with our minds is to read and meditate on God's Word daily. I don't mean the reading we do when we rush through it—like reading a book—but meditating and looking over the Word of God, the meanings of the words, and allowing the Word of God to speak to us, penetrate our minds, and settle in our hearts. It takes commitment and time to do this, so by setting a place and time, distractions are reduced to our benefit. It means rejecting the world's culture and way of thinking and embracing a kingdom culture based on biblical truths.

As we give our minds to the Holy Spirit, old, worldly mind-sets will be broken. ' God's Word says in Romans 12:2, "And do not be conformed to this world, but be transformed by the renewing of your mind, that you may prove what is that good and acceptable and perfect will of God." As we start to think and meditate on the things of the Spirit, the Holy Spirit begins the work of renewing our minds. This does not mean that old, negative, carnal thoughts won't come. But now we will be able to identify them and reject them by coming into agreement with the revealed Word of God placed in our hearts.

I recall one particular discouraging day where the Holy Spirit started to comfort me using Scripture.

I was refreshed, but this means whatever we put into our spirits and minds is what we get out of it. God speaks to us through the words with which we have fed our spirits. When words that contradict the Word of God rise up, we must gain the victory by "casting down arguments and every high thing that exalts itself against the knowledge of God, bringing every thought into captivity to the obedience of Christ" (2 Cor. 10:5).

For many of us who came to Christ out of the world, there is already much in our minds that is against God's will. Even as we try to renew our minds by filling them with the Word and will of God, these old things will pop up. The best way to deal with it is to simply let it pass by and not give life to the thought by dwelling on it. Worrying about the thought will only distract you and give it opportunity to grow roots and bring fruits of carnal behaviour. So when they come to mind, don't dwell on them. Let them just pass by.

With All My Soul

When we look into our loving God with our minds, everyone can clearly figure out that the focus must come from our intellect and thinking. When we try to love God from the soul, we'll find this to be a lot more difficult. In order to identify what the Bible means by loving God with all our souls, we must look at the Old Testament and New Testament meanings of the words. In the Old Testament, the Hebrew word for soul is *nephesh*, which means to breathe.[8] This is the breath of life that God breathes into man. The Greek word for soul in the New Testament is *psyche*, from which the word *psychology* is derived.[9] This covers everything to do with our will, passions, and desires. When looking at them together, our soul is our will and our choices developed from our passions and desires. In a more detailed sense, the soul describes our individual character and personality.

So loving God with all our soul means to love God with our decisions and with our personalities in the way we conduct ourselves and the way we speak. In this section, we are going to be looking at loving God with our speech, conducting ourselves in humility, and overlooking the wrongs of others as we love God with all our souls. Because of our sinful nature, our natural tendency is drawn to the proud nature we inherited from Adam after the fall. This pride even in its subtle and most unidentified form is fed by the world we see and by the social demands and pressures around us.

---

[8] http://www.biblestudytools.com/lexicons/hebrew/nas/nephesh.html

[9] http://biblehub.com/greek/5590.htm

In the kingdom of God it is different. We can clearly see humility, which is the opposite of pride and is the foundation of Jesus' ministry. He was born in a manger, not a palace or a place of prestige. Jesus Christ, God in the flesh, humbled Himself to take on flesh for our sakes.

> *Let this mind be in you which was also in Christ Jesus, who, being in the form of God, did not consider it robbery to be equal with God, but made Himself of no reputation, taking the form of a bondservant, and coming in the likeness of men. And being found in appearance as a man, He humbled Himself and became obedient to the point of death, even the death of the cross. (Phil. 2:5–8)*

The Bible tells us that we have to be imitators of Christ. This means taking off the arrogance and proud nature of the world and taking on the humble character of Jesus. We don't simply choose humility out of duty but as an expression of our love for God. As we look at Jesus' humility, we need to ask the Holy Spirit to impart that humility in our hearts. We need to seek God so we can love God in the same manner that Jesus loved God, being obedient even unto death. Jesus had a servant's heart; He washed the feet of His disciples. Can we even imagine this happening in this day and age? Imagine someone we hold in high esteem, humbling him or herself to wash the feet of others—

your feet. It is hard, isn't it? We might even feel embarrassed if he or she attempted to touch our feet because of how our feet look or because we are so lowly in comparison to someone so highly respected.

In the New Testament, Christ was always serving, healing the sick, raising the dead, and meeting the needs of others. Even when He was persecuted and had the power to stop it, He did not. He didn't say a word. In lowliness of heart, He humbled himself. Many of us, myself included, will defend ourselves verbally or physically, thinking we need to get justice. Even in little things, for example when someone says something wrong, we feel we need to automatically correct him or her. But how often is such correction spoken in the right way? Often times it will merely incite greater conflict. Humility would be to keep quiet, finding the right time to share the truth in love. Love seeks the best interests of others and does not seek its own (1 Cor. 13).

Sometimes the world identifies humility as weakness. Nevertheless, it takes a lot more strength to operate in humility. Humility is having the power to do something but restraining that power instead of unleashing it because of our love for God. Another word to use for humility is meekness, which is also defined as being peaceful, at rest, calm, and gentle.

These are all characteristics that we must possess to love God with all our souls.

Even when Jesus died on the cross, this was still deemed a curse (Gal. 3:10–13). Yet He humbled Himself. Even though dying on the cross was traumatic, people who had previously celebrated His miracles were now celebrating His death. What a humble experience for Jesus, carrying the cross in the midst of people who hated Him. But still, He did not react. He was innocent, but still He did nothing. He did not seek justification; He remained humble.

When we look at our own lives in light of Jesus, what would we have done? Would we fight? Would we defend ourselves? Would we seek justice? The answer for me would be yes. I want to get my view across. I would want to fight for my innocence. But for the love of God and for the love He had for us, Jesus humbled Himself. Jesus did not come to gain a name for Himself. He did everything in His Father's name.

> *John 5:19 says, "Then Jesus answered and said to them, 'Most assuredly, I say to you, the Son can do nothing of Himself, but what He sees the Father do; for whatever He does, the Son also does in like manner.'"*

He did not think or do anything unless the Father told Him to. He sought no honour or glory for Himself.

But in every action, He gave glory to His Father in heaven. We must behave in a way that is humble. This will come with practice, and at times, we may fail, but nevertheless we press on, seeking to love God with humility.

> *Meekness is an immovable state of the soul which remains unaffected whether in evil report or in good report, in dishonour or in praise.*
>
> —*Ladder of Divine Ascent*[10]

We need to be still both in the place of persecution and in the place of praise. We need to ask the Holy Spirit to do this in us and through us, so that we can put on Christ in different situations in our lives—at work, among friends or family, or in any situation where we feel like there is a form of injustice that has taken place. We have to forgive, and we also have to respond in love. Like all things, practice does make perfect.

---

[10] St John Climacus, *The Ladder of Divine Ascent* (New York: Harper & Brothers, 1959) 44.

Taming the Tongue

When we speak in a jesting manner, which is so common and normal in this culture, we often discover that the tongue can take us to places we didn't even anticipate. You want to fit in, so you say things that were better not said. Often when we've spoken too much, it is because we are showing off in front of our peers or want to amuse or be recognised. Yet these are all fruits of pride and not of humility. Humility seeks not to be seen but that God would be seen. We're all familiar with James 3:1–6 about taming the tongue. Let's read it:

> *My brethren, let not many of you become teachers, knowing that we shall receive a stricter judgment. For we all stumble in many things. If anyone does not stumble in word, he is a perfect man, able also to bridle the whole body. Indeed, we put bits in horses' mouths that they may obey us, and we turn their whole body. Look also at ships: although they are so large and are driven by fierce winds, they are turned by a very small rudder wherever the pilot desires. Even so the tongue is a little member and boasts great things. See how great a forest a little fire kindles! And the tongue is a fire, a world of iniquity. The tongue is so set among our members that it defiles the whole body, and sets on fire the course of nature; and it is set on fire by hell. (NKJV)*

This Scripture clearly speaks of the power of the tongue and our inability to tame it. It also speaks about the destruction the tongue brings and that a perfect man is a man who does not sin with his mouth. This is very important when we look at humility. Pride is often communicated verbally. As the *Ladder of Divine Ascent* states, "Talkativeness is the throne of vainglory."[11] It is when we speak that we are able to boast and show off. And as the proverb says, "In the multitude of words sin is not lacking, But he who restrains his lips is wise" (Prov. 10:19 NKJV). If we analyse all that is said about the tongue, we will realise how much we need to earnestly seek the Holy Spirit for Him to bridle our speech.

Many times a normal conversation with friends about our lives will stray. What started innocently ends with judgment of others, coarse jesting, and things not to be associated with professing Christians. In guarding our minds, we find that unless we guard our tongues, they are likely to lead our minds astray. We need to analyse our conversations, and as the Word says, we have to be slow to speak, we have to be careful with our words, and we must remember that the power of life and death are in the tongue (Prov. 18:21). Through our careless speech, we could commit a variety of sins that grieve the Holy Spirit, preventing us from loving God with our souls, our personalities, and our decisions.

---

[11] St John Climacus, *The Ladder of Divine Ascent* (New York: Harper & Brothers, 1959) 50.

Sometimes we deceive ourselves into thinking our gossip is okay or necessary. We really need to look and see what God requires of us in regard to our speech. We need to—for the love of God and our pursuit of Him—speak words that only edify others and glorify Him (Eph. 4:29–30). If we go back to the principle of consciously having Jesus with us wherever we go, then we will be aware that He hears every word of slander, gossip, pride, and so on. Not only do we offend the person we speak ill of and the one we are speaking to, but we also grieve the Holy Spirit of God. This means we must always seek to use our words to exemplify and express the love evident in 1 Corinthians 13.

In order to grow into greater intimacy with God, it is essential to be watchful at the gates of our mouths so that we utter a blessing and not a curse. As we bless people and "impart grace to others," God's presence is increased around us and becomes a blessing to the hearer as well. One of the more difficult tasks of controlling the tongue for me is that of not complaining. I always have something negative to say. The tea was too hot or too cold, too small or too big. It is a bad habit, and I'm praying I get delivered from it. God's Word says in Philippians 2:12–16 that we have to do things without complaining or disputing and to be blameless, without fault.

Refraining from talking also gives us the ability to be still inside and hear God while we are listening to others. In Henri Nouwen's book *The Way of the Heart*, he describes one of the benefits of silence as follows:

> *When the door of the steam bath is continually left open, the heat inside rapidly escapes through it; likewise the soul, in its desire to say many things, dissipates the remembrance of God through the door of speech, even though everything it says may be good. Thereafter the intellect, though lacking appropriate ideas, pours out a welter of confused thoughts to anyone it meets, as it no longer has the Holy Spirit to keep it free from fantasy…Timely silence, then, is precious, for it is nothing less than the mother of the wisest thoughts.*[12]

When we speak out of turn or even speak too much—which is actually birthed out of self-interest—we lose some of the fire that the Holy Spirit has activated in our lives. We have to live in a way that increases this fire and protects it, so we can have continuous communion with the Holy Spirit in love without it being hindered.

---

[12] Henri Nouwen, *The Way of the Heart* (New York: HarperCollins, 1981), 54.

With All My Heart

Loving God with all of our hearts means loving Him with our emotions, setting our hearts towards Him with love. This requires us to get to know God, study-ing and reading about Him and gaining more insight and knowledge about how He loves us. Expressing love back in return, as we pursue God in this manner, causes the Holy Spirit to assist in changing our hearts. We have set our love upon God in the same manner that David set his heart upon God (Ps. 91:14).

First, in order to love God with all our hearts, we must remove the idols that have already taken His place. These idols are different for everyone. For one person it could be vanity and for another it could be power and fame. Everybody has to seek the Holy Spirit to see what idols they have set up in God's place, asking God for the grace to remove them.

It is impossible to really love God with our hearts when they are already preoccupied with other things. Sometimes to determine what is actually in our hearts and what we actually value, we really have to look at the way we spend our time and money. This is a very good clue to show exactly where our hearts are. The Bible says:

For where your treasure is, there your heart will be also. The lamp of the body is the eye. If therefore your eye is good, your whole body will be full of light. But if your eye is bad, your whole body will be full of darkness. If therefore the light that is in you is darkness, how great is that darkness! No one can serve two masters; for either he will hate the one and love the other, or else he will be loyal to the one and despise the other. You cannot serve God and mammon. (Matt. 6:21–24)

We cannot desire the things of this world—money, fame, and power—and love God at the same time. As the Word says—whether we like it or not—"you will end up loving one and hating the other." In this case, God usually gets the short straw when people try to balance loving the things of the world and loving Him at the same time. If you think, "*Oh, this once won't hurt*," then we must realise how easy it is to deviate from the love and intimacy we once had with God. We have to consciously set our minds on God to love Him. This is a decision no one can make for you. David made the decision to set his heart upon God. Mary, in the New Testament, made a decision to set her heart upon God, listening at the feet of Jesus. She not only made a decision here, but she also invested her time and her money. Where her treasures were was where her heart was—with Jesus.

When people are in love, there is nothing they wouldn't do. That love drives them. It fuels them and gives them energy. In the natural world, we can readily identify people in love—the amount of time they spend together and the way they look into each other's eyes. Bystanders looking on know they're in love. The term *lovesick* is derived from the fact that a person's object of love is missing or away, and he or she feels sick over it. It is a deep yearning that results from missing the one he or she loves.

As we develop intimacy with God, setting our hearts to love Him day by day, we become so familiar and so at peace with the presence of God; it is something we may not even realise is happening. Eventually this will grow to the point where to be without it for a second will make us lovesick and withdrawn. It doesn't always feel nice, yet it's a blessing, because it is an indication that we are in love, unable to be apart from Jesus. This makes us more reluctant to do anything or behave in any way that would hinder our love relationship with God.

As we invest time, sitting at the feet of Jesus and meditating on His Word, we cultivate love. We will develop a more intimate relationship with Him as we make the commitment to love with all our hearts. The Holy Spirit, God's agent of change, empowers us to fulfill that commitment. As we pray and our desire to love God increases, the Holy Spirit changes us until we are in hot pursuit.

With All Our Strength

In this section, we will be exploring what it means to love God with all our strength. When looking at *Strong's Concordance*, loving God with all our strength means to love him with our resources, our ability, and all our might. This looks at our talents, our money, and our energy. It means living a life totally abandoned to God.

When we look through the Scriptures, we see so many passages that call us to reach out to the lame, the poor, the orphans, and the widows. We are to meet their needs and not to overlook them. This requires our strength—strength in resources and strength in time and commitment. We are also called to make disciples of men and share the gospel abroad. This too requires strength, resources, time, and commitment. As we love God, we discover a two-way benefit … not just for us but for others who are changed because of our love for God.

As we go, we represent His hands and legs on the face of the earth. When we give to God all our strength and money and love our neighbours, the Bible requires us to do it in secret, not looking for personal recognition or a name for ourselves. The Word of the Lord says in Matthew 6:3–4, "The father who sees in secret will Himself reward you openly" (NKJV). We need to do all our deeds for God and not for man.

When looking at loving God with our resources, this is not merely looking at financial resources. This can also include provisions like clothing, housing, and other forms of support. When loving God with these things, we express it through giving, not just out of our abundance but sometimes giving even out of our need.

For some people giving is the hardest thing you can ask them to do. This can be because of the ungodly relationship with money. Too often we forget that the resources in this world are all owned by God.

Nevertheless, like with all things concerning love, God requires that we give it voluntarily.

There are a variety of ways people can support others and add to the resources of the kingdom of God. This could be giving offerings and tithes. It could be through helping somebody you know is needy. It could be allowing someone destitute to use a spare room in your house. It could also be by supporting a food bank or going out your way to help people who are in prison or who are in need of support. In whatever way the Holy Spirit impresses us to give, we must give out of love and not duty. We also can't fall into the trap of giving with the hope of any return— whether financial or other benefits. We must simply give because we love God, love His purpose, and want to see His commission accomplished.

Giving also requires us to wrestle with greed for the things of this world. Regardless of what it may be—a hobby, cars, holidays, clothes—we will invest our resources in order to be able to do it. This is also true when we look at loving God and the things concerning His kingdom. If we love the kingdom of God and if we love God, we must also love contributing to the advancement of the kingdom of God in the lives of others.

Serving Others

Strangely enough, serving others as an expression of love to God is closely intertwined with giving of our resources. For instance, we might see someone who looks lonely and broken so we want to invite him or her for dinner. This not only requires us to spend time, give attention, and serve this person but also requires the resources to buy the food and to be able to make him or her feel welcome within our homes. I thank God for the people God has put into my life who have served me as an expression of love to God. I definitely wouldn't be where I am today. But for them I would probably be either dead or homeless. Serving others requires us to deny ourselves of our own needs to seek how we can meet the needs of others … who may be in greater need. Once again, we love God as we love others, and in doing so, we feel His loving heart while changing the lives of others at the same time.

There are examples all around the world of people who have used their lives to change the lives of others by serving. A very good example of this is Mother Teresa of Calcutta. Mother Teresa founded the Missionaries of Charity, a Roman Catholic religious congregation, which in 2012 consisted of over 4,500 sisters and is active in 133 countries. They run hospices and homes for people with HIV/AIDS, leprosy, and tuberculosis, soup kitchens, children's and family counselling programmes, orphanages, and schools. Members of the order must adhere to the vows of chastity, poverty, and obedience and to give "wholehearted and free service to the poorest of the poor."[13] Many may see her life as being quite lofty in regard to service–something they feel is personally un-attainable in regards to their own daily living and per-sonal commitments, but if we look around us, there is always something we can do, whether great or small. It's our hearts that God is after.

---

[13] (Wikipedia). http://en.wikipedia.org/wiki/Mother Teresa, last updated 4th November 2013.

Prayer and Fasting

Everybody who has attempted to pray for any length of time will find out that it requires strength, attention, and emotional fortitude to be able to seek God earnestly for ourselves and others. This must be done consistently in order to show an expression of love in regard to personal strength. When we set time aside to pray and study the Word, we are using our strength that we would have otherwise used doing other things. This brings God great delight as we choose Him first. Many times the reason we are unable to use our strength to pray consistently every day is because we haven't got a set time or place to be able to achieve this. To successfully achieve it, we have to be committed and consistent in the time spent.

Fasting to some people in contemporary Christianity is definitely considered a fossil. Fasting is a hidden treasure that is often overlooked and many times ignored. Nevertheless, the benefits of fasting can be seen right in the Bible. Jesus stated very clearly that certain people could not be set free unless it was through fasting and prayer (Matt. 17:19–21).

When we fast, it is not to gain brownie points with God. Fasting doesn't make God love us anymore than He already does. What fasting does is to position us to receive more from the Holy Spirit. As we fast, we lose physical strength, yet we are empowered by the Holy Spirit and gain an increased hunger and thirst for His presence and His righteousness. Fasting positions us to receive from God.

In fact, fasting will soften our hard hearts—a hardness that is developed through the culture of this world. Fasting enables us to spend more intimate time with God. Fasting is not just the abstinence of food but also replacing food, socialising or technology for spending time with God in His Word and in prayer and worship. There are a variety of ways people can fast, and I wholeheartedly recommend Derek Prince's books on fasting, as well as the Daniel fast (Daniel 10:2-3).

Fasting enables us to practice self-control. This self-control begins to benefit every other area of our lives as we develop a life of fasting. Fasting also makes us sensitive to the things of the Spirit. We give our strength as we intercede and fast for others, changing nations and communities for Christ.

CHAPTER THREE

Pursuit—Lost Treasure

When you lose something valuable, you become anxious and frustrated as you try to frantically find it. The harder it is to find, the more urgency you have. For example, if you lose your keys, you first look in the obvious places, but soon you are checking in unlikely places as you become desperate to locate them. You get on your knees look under the sofa and behind the cupboard, and start looking in places you have never ventured before.

All of a sudden, you spot something that looks like your keys, but if it isn't, your excitement is squashed, making you even more frustrated. Sometimes while you are searching, the phone may ring or someone may knock on the door, distracting you.

This pursuit of lost treasure is similar to our pursuit of God. Sometimes life and things that are not as important get in the way and distract us, snaring our focus and attention. Nevertheless, once this distraction ceases there still remains a deep sense of loss, especially when the lost object is very dear to our hearts. The strength of this feeling of loss draws us back into the search, looking once again for our treasure.

You always know when someone has lost something. You can see it. That person is focused and active in his or her search. When looking for spiritual treasure, you have to go through all the rubbish and "look from where you have fallen and return to your first love." We go back into the old, hidden places, hoping and searching for the first love, which we have lost, put down, or replaced. We begin to search, never satisfied with a counterfeit or a replacement such as drugs, lust, or other distractions.

Many of us continue our searches, even silently, despite the ridicule from people who are no longer searching themselves. This is a treasure hunt, and our treasure is Jesus. Sometimes we get frustrated and stop looking, thinking there is no point and life goes on as usual. However, when we see something that even resembles what we lost, we check it just in case.

My own relationship with God was very much like that. I remember being on fire for God, full of passion and zeal. I was in love, but slowly things of the world pushed out my first priority of seeking the kingdom of God, and nothing else worked. What made it worse is that I felt spiritually low. I was lovesick and could feel in my spirit and my life that something had gone drastically wrong. The Holy Spirit had departed. Many of us delude ourselves—as I did—that the Holy Spirit will work with us even in disobedience. Others still believe that compromise and lack of spiritual growth is covered by the grace of God, overlooking that it is written: "Should we sin because grace abounds, certainly not." Don't misunderstand me. As

Christians, we fall daily, and His grace, mercy, and compassion are still present as He is a loving Father and will love us and pick us up. If your two-year-old child throws food off the table, you would have compassion and understanding as he progressively grows and takes responsibility. However, if your seventeen-year-old continued to do the same thing, you would be very concerned—unless of course, the child has special needs.

In the dark, a counterfeit object can look very real, until the light of God shines on it. Then it does not resemble the true treasure. I remember looking for one of my earrings. As I was going up the stairs, I turned the lights off and instantly saw something in the shadows that looked like my earring, but the moment I flipped the light back on, I realised to my disappointment that it was just a small piece of wood.

Just like modern church, when the lights are turned off and the music fades, we are simply left with a building, a PA system, and hungry souls suffering from malnutrition. This is so evident in the way we live our lives from day to day. We are no longer seeking the treasure and find ourselves satisfied with the counterfeit we have found (that which cannot save). Many attending church regularly have already died in the spirit. They are now the living dead, living in the world but completely unaware of and dead to the things of the spirit. Our brothers and sisters in Christ know they are in a serious situation since God, who is so gracious, does not allow us to be satisfied until we find our way home. In fact, for true children of God, there will be a feeling of lovesickness, a dullness of spirit.

Many in this situation want to be restored, want to reconnect with God but do not have the spiritual knowledge of their condition or the strength to get themselves out of the spiritual malaise they are in. But God, who so loves His children, raises watchmen who weep and cry day and night on behalf of God's people throughout each age to wake up the sleeping saints and resurrect the ones who are now all but spiritually dead.

One of the worst epidemics in Christianity is being able to read the Bible yet being so spiritually deaf and blind to the things God says and furthermore requires of us in our daily walk with Him. We have it, but we don't believe in it. A good example is what the Bible says about our words and how we speak. This doesn't prevent us—under the guise of sharing—from casually gossiping. If we do truly believe the Bible and all it says in our hearts, we wouldn't live half as worldly as we do.

God has blinded us, and yes, it is God who afflicts us as we daily afflict Him with our sins and our unacknowledged backsliding and refuse to take correction. We have stiffened our necks, our hearts have been hardened, and we are no longer sensitive to the things of God.

Some of us had the treasure of His presence. Oh what joy it is! All we wanted was to please Him and dwell with Him. But we allowed it to slip away and replaced it with the things of the world, through the busyness of life. Things without eternal value; things that look very desirable are fleeting in this present age. Others know the presence is gone and discuss the experience of loss with anyone who will listen without actively seeking out that which was lost. Things that glitter and satisfy the cravings of our flesh—the pride of life, such as the house, the car, the home, the business, the busy schedule, power, and prestige—have replaced our once-valued treasure.

The coldness of our hearts was gradual. There were those who were called as intercessors, who spent hours at the feet of God, praying, crying, and interceding. They wouldn't do anything before they sought the face of God. But now, through gradually living lives that don't allow space for God, the fellowship with the Holy Spirit—the cultivation of the secret place where intimacy takes place—has diminished. There were others called as evangelists who used to make a habit of speaking about Christ with those they met on a daily basis because the zeal of the Lord's house sat heavy on their souls. Now, when amongst people, they never mention Christ as their spirits have been dulled by things of this world.

The things of this world—even the seemingly normal and harmless ones—have managed to squeeze God into a Sunday service. For many, they just want to recover from a hard week's work and would rather meet with friends than with God. The Bible makes the battle between the spirit and the flesh over our souls so clear. But like teenagers whose parents warn them against a particular friend, we abandon good advice to the detriment of our souls.

When I was growing up in the church, living in the world meant choosing the things that were associated with the world. Today you can go to church and live just as you would in the world, facing little or no challenge about your eternal destination. While the things of this world satisfy our carnal nature, they have no eternal value and actually erode the seeds of righteousness operating in our lives.

What the world offers seems pleasurable and exciting, but they still fail to satisfy, and their pleasures soon wane, increasing the desire for more. In fact, the things of the world encourage our flesh to seek pleasure and relief in more vices. This offers only a false sense of enlightenment and relief. This too being a lie leaves the victim bound to this world with spiritual shackles, blindness and turning the mill like Samson: (Judges 16:v21). The flesh and the world are truly hard taskmasters.

Let's go back to my lost earring; it was a small black rose, costing probably seventy pence, but, it was the one I wore most of the time. I searched numerous times; finally, I just gave up and put some other ones on. I didn't understand where it could have gone. Interestingly, it was after I had given up my fruitless search that I still found myself unconsciously but actively searching for it. True Christians, despite having their spirits grow cold or lukewarm and losing the peace and the joy they once had with the Lord Jesus, still search for a cure. Just like the woman with the issue of blood, they have gone to many spiritual physicians but with little change.

Vices that we have unwittingly fallen in love with—even harmless ones to the natural eye—will reduce our ability to seek or want God, hindering our spiritual growth. They blind us, make us fall asleep in an attempt to steal our promised eternal destination with God. This is a loss that is very possible if we don't gird up our loins, depend on the strength of Christ, and cry out for personal revival.

Brokenness is the beginning of personal restoration of our intimacy with God. My heart was so hardened by the things of the world. They looked harmless to me and just a part of my everyday life, but the pride of life of having a big house, a big car, and everything new and modern had a serious impact on my walk with God. I had to work hard for these things that kept me pretty busy. I would justify it by saying, "But you know God understands." I was no longer living in the Spirit, even though I would go to church and feel His presence and anointing in the praise and worship. The secret place I once had—the fun, jokes, and love I had with the Holy Spirit—had gone.

I knew I needed to be active to get myself out of this pit. I read books about great men and women of God that inspired me to come up higher and make a difference in my generation—by the grace of God. I noticed a recurring trait in all of their lives: prayer. Some spent hours at night in His presence. In comparison, I was definitely on the wrong side of the cross.

I purposed in my heart and committed to pray early in the morning, but I could feel the blockage, a hardness that didn't make my approach easy. I recalled, as a new believer that I had once spent hours in prayer, which was such a joy and delight, but now something had changed. I felt like my prayer was hitting the ceiling and falling back down on me.

We all have close friends. But if you only ever spent a mere half-hearted thirty minutes a day with your friend, you would find yourself becoming distant. If you always seemed preoccupied with other things on your mind and were constantly looking at your watch, you would seem to be telling them that you wanted to leave. At times like this it is a picture of the relationship we have with God. We come to prayer because we believe it is our religious duty to commune in His presence, even though His presence is no longer there. Since we can't desire two opposing things, our love for the things of the world and a heart-felt love for God.

God requires us to love Him with everything. To be honest, I did love Him, but other things unknown to me had taken His place in my heart. This was evident in my Christian walk as the passion I once had was gone. Many Christians explain this as just part of the process—the honeymoon period is over. But if we stay connected to Jesus and allow His life to flow through us, the zeal and passion become evident and are rekindled. Loss of passion and a vibrant spirit are evidence that something is wrong. In this dangerous state, I found a book on holiness with prayer points that changed my life and my situation.

I'm sure, if you're willing to gain that which the devil has or is trying to steal, these prayers are simple. I have personally witnessed only a few people who really want to give their whole lives to God. Most people seem to be quite happy living and enjoying the things of this world and walking according to the dictates of the flesh. They are of this world, and there is no evident struggle towards intimacy to be at home with God.

God said in His Word that we must leave everything and follow Him (Matt. 16:24). Many of us who profess Christ are unwilling to give our lives into His hands. In fact, we don't mind having Christ and believing in Him. But we don't want any change or adjustment in our lives. We are unwilling to surrender everything under the lordship of God or change our habits and lifestyles to fit His agenda. We want Christ, but everything else to. In basic terms, we want to have our cake and eat it. This is called sitting on the fence, and the devil owns the fence. God's Word warns us about being double-minded. He has called us to be single-minded. If we decide we want to do it our way, then we are walking in disobedience, which is a sin. As we draw nearer to rebellion, God darkens our hearts, preventing us from ever coming home, except through humility. Only with true repentance, earnest hunger, and thirsting for the righteousness of God can we see change and restoration.

It is so sad that so many will be unable to receive this word because they are so used to having a gospel that they only take from, where there is nothing required in return. Some of us are still very much in love with our idols that we make any excuse, deceiving ourselves that everything is great with us spiritually.

The Bible says we should examine ourselves. This doesn't mean only using our eyes and our understanding of things. The Bible says, "The heart is deceitful above all things, and desperately wicked…"(Jeremiah 17:9) We all have a more favourable view of ourselves than we actually are. Ask the Holy Spirit to reveal to you the condition of your heart. This will be very delicate surgery, and in fact, we need to ask God daily to open our spiritual eyes and ears. We must ask God to remove the scales from our eyes and everything in our lives that has come to steal away our love and intimacy with God. Before we even start these prayers, there has to be a conscious lifelong commitment to pursue God. Otherwise we will end the journey before we've begun. We have to commit to spending time with God in prayer and in His Word. Again, it takes work. It's painful, but yes, it's all so worth it. When it comes to treasure, the seekers do not want to be distracted until they have found what they have lost. They want to focus and retrace their steps in the hope of locating that which has been lost. God helped me find my lost treasure; He helped me find my way home. This is what God is waiting for us to do, to get so frustrated with ourselves in our search that we cry out to Him like little children to take us from the choking shackles of the world. It is this heartfelt cry of brokenness that brings us to our knees, flat on our faces in total surrender and dependency. Only when we ask God will we recover all that has been lost. Only when we come with broken hearts to a merciful God will He come and heal our backsliding. This is the humility God is looking for, the singleness of mind that is a focused, unmoved, unrelenting pursuit in search of the great treasure of the regained intimacy with God; friendship, love, and peace. This will give us a greater appreciation for His love and His grace.

All of us must identify areas where we have strayed, where our walk has become church as usual … yet our hearts are unchanged. We have to search our lives and seek out where we lost our treasure, our first love. "What came to hinder you from doing well?"(Gal. 5:7) We need to earnestly search this out with all our hearts, not in a lukewarm, half-hearted manner, as if it is just another church programme. God's Word says "He will cut us off if we are not connected to the vine" (John 15:2). However, He will prune us if we allow Him to take away the things that hinder our love. Some of those things we may hold so dearly to our hearts that they have now become deep-rooted idols. They have replaced God's position and have also taken away the hunger and thirst we once had for the things of God. We are now dull and want nothing more because we are already full of the things we have crowded into our lives.

We need to constantly examine ourselves, looking again, seeking again, and searching again. If we were given a pile of unorganised papers, we would have to go through each of them and analyse them in detail to determine how best to organise them. This takes time, focus, patience, and attention. In the same way, we must take time and have patience to rid our hearts of the things that hinder our relationship with God. And this we must do if we are to be released from the spiritual shackles that hinder our growth and ultimately determine our eternal destination. "Rend your heart and not your garments" (Joel 2:13 NKJV).

Once Saved Always Saved

"Not everyone who says to me, 'Lord, Lord', shall enter the kingdom of heaven, but he that does the will of my father in heaven. Many will say to Me in that day, 'Lord, Lord have we not prophesied in Your name, cast out demons in Your Name, and done many wonders in Your name?' And then I will declare to them, 'I never knew you; depart from Me, you who practice lawlessness." (Matt. 7:21–23 NKJV)

Some Christians believe that once they have given their lives to Christ they are promised eternal life no matter how they live or conduct themselves. The above Scriptures clearly show that there will be many who come and give Jesus an account of the work they believe they were doing for the kingdom, as if they believe this was a valid reason and evidence that they should go in. These people are people who not only believed they were Christians but were also ministers of the gospel. This can be seen in their description: "We prophesied in your name, cast out demons in your name, and done many wonders in your name."

I mean, picture it. It's judgment day, and all the professing Christians are lining up, convinced they were Christians on earth and are no doubt getting in. I would be singing, dancing, and so excited to get in. Then all of a sudden, in the presence of Jesus, the Saviour of the world, I would fall silent, being speechless at the magnitude of the moment when He said, "I never knew you. Depart from Me, you who practiced lawlessness!"

The thing about this scene for me is that the people who were speaking to Christ were unaware that they would not get in. I'm only guessing and trying to use my imagination here, but they probably begged Jesus to let them in. They obviously thought He had made a mistake. One man in that company probably recalled his Christian life and commitments and everything he had done for the kingdom. He was raised in a Christian home, went to Bible school, spent his whole life in the church, committed to the work of God, counselled couples, ministered the Word, and represented Christ on earth. Another person would say, "But I went to church every Sunday and gave all I could. I volunteered in my local charity and read my personal daily devotional." They will be in total bewilderment and confusion that Jesus said they can't enter in.

I thank God that we are on the other side of this experience with the opportunity to truly examine ourselves by looking at our lives in their entirety, looking at both major and minor areas where we have erred. These people did not enter the kingdom of God because they didn't believe. The Bible said that even the demons believe (James 2:19). But these people never knew God and they practiced lawlessness (they were transgressors).

Knowing someone and reading about someone are two different things. One of my closest friends, Karen, knows me very well—the way I talk and walk, the things I like and hate—and we share things that people would never know about me unless they had a personal relationship with me. There are also people who may have read about me or seen my public face, but they only know *about* me; they don't know me. Their knowledge is based upon second-hand information and not on an experiential relationship.

Matthew 7:21 clearly confirms that a person could minister to people even manifest the gifts of the Spirit and still be without repentance and actually not know God. I have witnessed way too many services and heard minsters teach on an experience they have never had, and unfortunately, it shows. You will know when you see someone who has met with God. The way people talk about a friend they are intimate with is totally different from the way they speak about someone they have never met. They bring a piece of God with them. As you listen, it is as if you can touch a piece of that intimacy and silently long to share and have what they are talking about.

Getting to know Jesus for real, not merely from a book or preaching or the numerous resources this generation has available to gain head knowledge about Him, is what it's all about. To personally know Christ in a daily intimate relationship is essential to entering the kingdom of heaven. From the passage above, we can clearly see that giving your life to Christ at one time in your life and then backing it up with good help, ministry, and everything else defined as the work of God will just not stand in the end. We have to pursue a deeper relationship with God beyond the crowd, beyond the music, and beyond the coffee mornings we have.

The Greatest Commandment

"Teacher, which is *the great commandment in the law?" Jesus said to him, '"You shall love the* LORD *your God with all your heart, with all your soul, and with all your mind.' This is* the *first and great commandment. Matthew 22:36-38 (NKJV)*

The first commandment is one of the most over-looked commandments, yet God still requires it of us.

Do you love God with everything? This is a se-rious question because in the end God will be judging us on exactly that, and I think it would be wise for us to take a good look at our lives before answering that question. The Bible tells us that where our treasure is, that is where our heart will be also. Do a complete in-ventory of your life and how you spend your week and your money. How do you truly invest in this relation-ship with God and invest in eternity? Or are you simp-ly investing in the church and meeting your friends? These may seem like tasking questions, but I would rather hear these words from a fool like me than to stand in front of a mighty God and be told I'm not coming in.

Modern Christianity

We really need to ask God to open our spiritual eyes and ears because the Word says, "The lamp of the body is the eye. If therefore your eye is good, your whole body will be full of light. But if your eye is bad, your whole body will be full of darkness. If therefore the light that is in you is darkness, how great *is* that darkness!" (Matt. 6:22–23 NKJV). I sit here totally broken and in tears, and I pray that God will put us all on the right path and wake us up from the counterfeit gospel that has blinded us and caused us to fall asleep to the real, heartfelt things of God. Many churches today are not preaching the God evident in the Bible, but a God who will accept us just as we are, with our idols and no spiritual growth.

Yes, God does say come as you are, and no change in our lives is by our power or might but simply by His grace and mercy. But He does expect us to grow from glory to glory until we reach the full stature of Christ. This message of "come as you are and stay as you are" is very attractive to the world. Everybody loves Jesus as long as we don't have put down our toys. We have created a god made with our own hands, that we can put in our pockets. When negative circumstances come or we need a little extra help, we take Him out and use Him as a cash card to fulfill our every whim.

What a sad condition of our modern-day churches! Many minsters know the truth, yet they fear speaking the truth because they know their congregations are in love with their idols. The truth written in the Word about repentance and our eternal options—not just the lovely bits but the bits that truly challenge the condition of people's hearts—are hardly ever heard from our pulpits. Even worse, people have been fed such a watered-down version of the Bible, mixed with everything else the world could offer, that when sermons that challenge the way people live are shared, the message is said to be too tough on people. We either hear the hard truth now when we can actually seek God and do something about it or hear it from God when we can't.

Satan loves our churches because instead of maintaining biblical foundations and the discipleship of the saint, we have decided to seek the world's view of how to do God's work. I'm totally and utterly confused on how that works. Instead of us fleeing the world, as the Bible instructs us to (James 4:4, 2 Timothy 4:10, 1 John 2:15 – 16), we have now decided to sleep with the enemy.

We have become worldly in our service and relationship with God. We have thrown out the prayer meetings, fasting, and night vigils and replaced them with concerts and shows readily available in the world

… No wonder the world doesn't seriously consider joining the church. We have actually lost our way. We haven't merely lost our first love; we decided to marry His archenemy. Then we wonder why it is so difficult to pray effectively, why our testimonies are so feeble, and why we look nothing like the Christ we profess but more like the world we serve and have come into bondage with.

What a dire situation we are in. As a body of believers, where we are so godless and religious, "having a form of godliness but denying the power therein." We are surely living in the time spoken about in 2 Timothy 4:3–4. Paul says, "For the time will come when they will not endure sound doctrine, but according to their own desires, because they have itching ears, they will heap up for themselves teachers; and they will turn their ears away from the truth and be turned aside to fables" (NKJV).

How well this describes the condition of the church. We seem to have fallen asleep with the deluded idea that we all get to heaven even when we have been living like the world with no continuous personal preparation for eternity. We have been too busy dealing with secondary things like projects and buildings that have no weight whatsoever in the eternal scheme of things.

Many Christians are in this situation and are unable to break free. God has blinded their eyes because of pride, which has led to self-righteousness. Yes, many of us have had true encounters with God, where He revealed Himself in our lives, but that was ten years ago. What is happening now? In Romans 1:18–32, this condition of knowing God and still living a life of lawlessness is discussed in more detail.

Spiritual Blindness

Many Christians who read this book will no doubt say to themselves, "That's not me. That sounds like so-and-so." We get to a place where we become spiritually blind to the truth, unable to see or discern the reality even when it is clearly before our eyes. To add insult to injury the blind individuals actually believe that they are seeing—just like the Pharisees referred to in the Scripture. The Pharisees were called blind leaders of the blind (Matt. 15:14, 23:23, 26). I've always said, from my own experience, that a minister can take you no further than he has been himself.

The cause of spiritual blindness in believers is spiritual pride and lukewarmness. This is made so clear to the prosperous church of Laodicea in Revelation 3:13–22:

"And to the angel of the church of the Laodiceans write, 'These things says the Amen, the Faithful and True Witness, the Beginning of the creation of God: "I know your works, that you are neither cold nor hot. I could wish you were cold or hot. So then, because you are lukewarm, and neither cold nor hot, I will vomit you out of My mouth. Because you say, 'I am rich, have become wealthy, and have need of nothing'—and do not know that you are wretched, miserable, poor, blind, and naked—I counsel you to buy from Me gold refined in the fire, that you may be rich; and white garments, that you may be clothed, that the shame of your nakedness may not be revealed; and anoint your eyes with eye salve, that you may see. As many as I love, I rebuke and chasten. Therefore be zealous and repent. Behold, I stand at the door and knock. If anyone hears My voice and opens the door, I will come in to him and dine with him, and he with Me. To him who overcomes I will grant to sit with Me on My throne, as I also overcame and sat down with My Father on His throne. He who has an ear, let him hear what the Spirit says to the churches.""" (NKJV)

In examining the message to the church of Smyrna, we find something interesting. The message is: "I know your works, tribulation, and poverty (but you are rich)" (Rev. 2:9 NKJV). The Smyrna church was spiritually rich because of their physical condition of being poor and persecuted. This was completely different from the Laodicean church, which had become rich and wealthy physically while believing they needed nothing from God.

When we have reached a level of wealth, there is a very real danger of becoming so preoccupied with the accumulation of wealth and the reputation that comes with it that we have little or no time to invest in the things of God. Our financial increase has a negative effect, causing us to be lukewarm and lose our hunger and love of Jesus. The wealthy church didn't only forget God, but their love for others beyond their circle also went cold. They were now ineffective in ministry because they were disconnected from the vine. People should not mistake numbers and programms for evidence of fruitfulness. Most churches in this situation are not even aware of their condition and are quite happy going on with church as usual without a deeper inspection of the condition of their hearts in the light of the Word of God.

I have personally experienced this dynamic myself and have seen how destructive it is to my relationship with God. When I first met God, we were inseparable. I attended every prayer meeting and studied and prayed every night. I had met the love of my life, and it was evident in every area. I walked with Him and talked with Him. In fact, I knew what it was to be walking in the Spirit. I wanted nothing at all to do with the world and even cut ties with my old friends from the old life. By God's grace, I stopped smoking and drinking and lived a life of fasting, praying, and seeking the face of God. I was either at church, at work, or at home. I would evangelise on the bus and the streets. I was mesmerised with my Saviour. My life consisted simply of me and God, and I ministered to others as the opportunity came. These were some of the best times in my spiritual walk. I was born again and loving it—loved everything about church and waiting on His Word to get direction for my every move. God was truly real to me. He was my friend. We walked together, joked together, and danced together. He provided for my every need, and He was all I needed.

I don't know where I lost the vibrant spirit I had developed when I had just met God. I was in love, and no one could take me from His presence. I was all His, my thoughts, my mind, everything. I was extreme at times but always passionate. I was lovesick, and it was evident. I was totally sold out for Him. I would do anything to be with Him and would see His face daily in prayer, worship, the Word, and charity. This communion was as real as any human relationship, but it was better. It was with the love of my soul.

Through the passion I had for God, I wanted to make a difference in the lives of the disadvantaged and marginalised people within the community— especially young teenage boys and girls who would otherwise be running around wild on the streets in gangs or wind up homeless … as I did at the age of seventeen. I set up a charity to help them, but as the charity profile increased through the national press and I engaged with local and central politicians, all manner of things began to change. I would get home too late to pray, being exhausted from the charity and two other businesses I ran. I had little or no time with God. I would squeeze in one hour with Him when I could, but my mind and body where somewhere else because I had so many other responsibilities. Even though I did know that my walk with God was declining, in my mind (which is the worst place to look), I thought God would understand all the demands and pressures of my job. He would realise the responsibilities I had to deal with. He would surely understand.

I still continued to go to church on Sundays and to midweek services when possible. I would feel the anointing in the service and always came home feeling refreshed. But deep inside my heart, I could see that there was clearly a blockage and a hindrance. To be honest, I thought overall I was spiritually okay, and yes I fell, but God is merciful. I never, ever thought or even considered that the way I was living would have such a dramatic effect on my spirit life that I would go so far away from God. I mean, was that even possible? I can see now that I was spiritually blind to my condition. My heart had hardened, and God was not at all happy with my lukewarmness and the compromise with my walk. Spiritual blindness can create white lies that the little sins of control and anger have no eternal weight, but they do—whether we are blind to it or not.

Wake-Up Call

I made a conscious decision in my heart to get out of this situation. I could feel the blockage between me and God, and my walk with God had become so casual, that I felt sick inside—lovesick. My soul had clear evidence that it was separated from God, and nothing but God could repair it. In the past I would wake up at five o'clock in the morning and spend time with God, but this was now a thing of the past. I decided I needed to pray through these barriers. The answer to these prayers was the end of one season of my life and the beginning of my true walk with God. The experience was a true eye-opener, and boy was it painful.

First of all, my husband started to see another woman. He was always on the phone with her. He would leave the house and come home late, telling me that he had met with one of his business partners. My heart was just being ripped out of my chest. I remember lying down on my office floor—where I had begun to sleep—and crying out to God, saying, "Look what is happening in my life!"

To my surprise, God responded, "Yes, you now know how I feel." He continued to speak to me, telling me that everything that was happening to me was everything I had been doing to Him. "I've given you everything, and you've turned your back on Me. I came to the places we used to meet, and you are nowhere to be found." I got it. It's like watching your best friend go off and spend time with someone else, as if you never existed. That is how I made God feel. I was broken. I cried to console myself, and I cried because I had abandoned God and was blinded to my current spiritual condition.

At this point, I—who had successfully given up drinking and smoking when I met God—started to drink heavily, trying to numb the pain and fill the gap that only God could fill. I would drink a bottle of fortified British wine every day, which caused me to fall asleep. But through this period I found God's grace and love steadfast. Six months before this point, I found a job opening in an area I loved. Everyone I told was against it, not knowing how much I was struggling running my own business. I got the job, but it was six months before I could begin. This is one of the things that God used to keep me alive. I had no more motivation or courage to work for myself. I was broken. The only thing that got me up in the mornings was the fact that I was now accountable to someone else, for which I thank God.

I closed up shop on everything. I left the house and went to stay with an older church lady. Just writing about this brings back the tears to my eyes. But I thank God because this was the way back into His presence. I often mentioned to my dear friend Karen that life is full of snakes and ladders, but the funny thing is the snakes on earth are actually spiritual ladders. The ladders on earth—the things like power, authority, and the things we believe will give us a good reputation or recognition—are actually spiritual snakes. They rob us of our humility, which we need to seek God. They take away our dependence on God for everything, increasing our pride and creating a gulf between us and God. This makes things worse as we are already filled with the things of the world and subsequently cannot hunger and thirst for His righteousness. It was at this point that I truly had to give my life back to God and no longer live it in my understanding but live it as directed by God. Living eternally minded was a lifelong practice that I needed to pursue to keep me on the right track.

Kingdom Lifestyle

The Sermon on the Mount is a sermon Jesus gave in Matthew 5–7, and I find it to be a very good overview of what is pleasing to God and how we should live our lives fully dedicated and committed to Him.

> *Blessed are the poor in spirit, For theirs is the kingdom of heaven. Blessed are those who mourn, For they shall be comforted. Blessed are the meek, For they shall inherit the earth. Blessed are those who hunger and thirst for righteousness, For they shall be filled. Blessed are the merciful, For they shall obtain mercy. Blessed are the pure in heart, For they shall see God. Blessed are the peacemakers, For they shall be called sons of God. Blessed are those who are persecuted for righteousness' sake, For theirs is the kingdom of heaven. Blessed are you when they revile and persecute you, and say all kinds of evil against you falsely for My*

sake. Rejoice and be exceedingly glad, for great is your reward in heaven, for so they persecuted the prophets who were before you. (Matt. 5:3–12 NKJV)

Poor in Spirit

You can clearly see, if God opens your eyes, how antithetical the world's culture is to the culture of the kingdom of God. Notice verse 3: "Blessed are the poor in spirit, for theirs is the kingdom of heaven." The culture of the world says, "Get rich or die trying." Riches are for the use and the display of this world.

We sometimes deceive ourselves. We may have started a charity or a Bible study group, but even these innocent things can become idols and take us away from the things of God. In the kingdom, the poor in spirit are the ones who inherit the kingdom of heaven. In my own life and in my general observation, it is hard to be rich in the world and still be poor in spirit. I found a survey that said that the people in the UK who are living on the poverty line are still in the richest 6.6 percent of the world's population (www.givingwhatwecan.org). A homeless, poor person is hungry and thirsty and is therefore humbled by his or her situation, begging for provision. Spiritually speaking, it is the same. The poor in spirit is the one who is unable to be holy as God requires. He sees what God's best is and is aware of his inability to make it happen. He needs the fruit of the Spirit in Galatians 5:22–23:

> *But the fruit of the Spirit is love, joy, peace, longsuffering, kindness, goodness, faithfulness, gentleness, self-control. Against such there is no law.*

This man knows that of his flesh he can do no good thing. A person who is poor in the spirit has sorrow in their heart, because they see that the Word says there are characteristics that are not supposed to be evident in a person's life who is professing Christ. He therefore wrestles and struggles daily in prayer, seeking God to give him that which he cannot provide for himself: victory over the flesh. This victory is promised in Isaiah 57:15:

> *For thus says the High and Lofty One Who inhabits eternity, whose name is Holy: "I dwell in the high and holy place, With him who has a contrite and humble spirit, To revive the spirit of the humble, And to revive the heart of the contrite ones." (NKJV)*

In response to our spiritual poverty, God revives us, and His strength is made perfect in our weakness (2 Cor. 12:9).

The rich in spirit are too full of the things of the world, becoming spiritually blind to their current spiritual state. They go to church, have a lovely time, and thank God for the great things He is doing in their lives. They are totally worldly focused, with just a sprinkle of Christianity to go with it. It is a form of godliness that indulges in the here and now. These things have stolen the greatest treasure of all: humility, the understanding that, without God, I can do absolutely nothing. Humility is the foundation of everything given in the spirit and the opposite—pride—is developed and nurtured in the world.

Those Who Mourn

It's a poor man who cries and mourns. It is a poor man who, because he is poor in the things of God and the things of the Spirit, cries out, "Father, help me! Deliver me from this flesh and this world." But a man who is in love with the world and all it brings him— the reputation, the house, the car, the respect, the security and the fulfilment of all fleshly desires, living with no accountability to God—has nothing to cry out to God for, because his flesh and soul are satisfied.

Indeed, such a man may not even be earning a great deal of money, but he still has no real desire or need for the things of God because he is already full with the things of the world. His condition of being content with the things of the world has blinded him to the fact that he has now become "you who practice lawlessness" and will not enter the kingdom of heaven. There is no middle ground. We are both mourning and seeking God to fill the gap in our spirits so that God's holiness can be revealed in our lives or we're living out the deeds of the flesh with the delusion that, on judgment day, we will not be accountable for how we truly lived. You see, unlike man, God does not judge appearances. God judges the heart. God is also not mocked. What a man sows he will reap.

We understand this principle when it comes to the things of the world, but we ignore it through blindness when it comes to the things of the Spirit. My sister is always telling her eldest son, Mario, "If you don't study hard, you will not get into a good school." She is teaching him that if he sows studying, discipline, and hard work, he will reap good grades and a good education. Some doctors are in school for up to sixteen years of their lives to become surgeons. We know, earthly speaking, that if we want to get a career, we have to train and gain experience. We sow our time, our money, our strength, our family time, our God times, and all our resources to be able to gain something that will cease to exist in one hundred years.

We don't even use one hundredth of that same effort to seek God for the power of the Holy Spirit in order to see godly changes in our lives. We seriously don't think we can get to heaven with this lukewarm approach … based on a prayer we made ten years ago but that has not borne any fruit in the last five years. When we are following the culture of the world and there is no urgency about the condition of our hearts and souls, there is no fruit. We saw earlier how a minister tried to enter but couldn't because he did not know God and because he practiced lawlessness. Walking after the deeds of the flesh produces fruits of lawlessness, however respectable the sins may be.

The Meek

The word *meek* means humble and submissive[14]. Our greatest example of this is in the life of Jesus Christ. "Let this mind be in you which was also in Christ Jesus, who, being in the form of God, did not consider it robbery to be equal with God, but made Himself of no reputation, taking the form of a bondservant, *and* coming in the likeness of men. And being found in appearance as a man, He humbled Himself and became obedient to *the point of* death, even the death of the cross. Therefore God also has highly exalted Him and given Him the name which is above every name." (Phil. 2:5–9 NKJV).

We are supposed to be imitators of Christ, and one of the great characteristics He possessed was a humble spirit. Everything Jesus had, He borrowed from someone else. He possessed nothing, not even the tomb He was briefly buried in. Jesus Christ was rich, but for our sake, He became poor. He is the creator of the whole universe, but because of love, He wrapped Himself in humility, in human flesh so He could bring us back home. What a wonderful and gracious God we have, that through His poverty, we might be made rich (2 Cor. 8:9). He humbled Himself, not so we can gain earthly riches but to gain heavenly

---

[14] http://www.thefreedictionary.com/meek

riches and a heavenly home. Throughout Jesus' three-year ministry, He borrowed everything He needed. He was even born in a manger, surrounded by animals. What a humble beginning for the King of Kings. Yet in all this, He lived a life of simplicity that spoke about a heavenly kingdom and how we must get in. Jesus' life was a life of humility, and it is a life we must all embrace and seek if we are to grow into intimacy with God.

Humility dies to self and depends on God for everything. The Holy Spirit is simply waiting for us to give Him the keys to our being through humility so He can completely own us and fulfil His will through our whole lives. In the words of Andrew Murray in His book *Humility: The Journey toward Holiness*:

> *If this be the root of the tree, its nature must be seen in every branch and leaf and fruit. If humility be the first, the all including grace of the life of Jesus, if humility be the secret of His atonement, then the health and strength of our spiritual life will entirely depend upon our putting this grace first too, and making humility the chief thing we admire in Him, the chief thing we ask of Him, the one thing for which we sacrifice all else.*[15]

Humility and seeing our inability to do things without God are the keys to accessing all other graces and vir-

---

[15] Andrew Murray, *Humility: The Journey toward Holiness* (Minneapolis, MN: Bethany House, 2001), 11.

tues from God. The spirit of the world distributes this freely with the positions, reputations, and things we acquire. We live in a generation where we're celebrated and defined by what we possess, the car we drive, the job we have, even the postal code where we live, and our social network. The Spirit is totally different. The world says we've got to have this and that, and because we worked for it, we become proud and conceited— our hearts continually going further and further away from God.

Just looking at these three characteristics established in the Sermon on the Mount, we should be able to identify that there is something hindering our walk with God. Now we have to seek God for Him to change us.

The Pruning Process

It's simply crazy. When I met God, I thought that I needed Him. I mean I've always needed Him, but at this point, if he didn't rescue me from the life I was living, I would end up dead. I thank God for His grace. I knew that when God's Word says our relationship goes from glory to glory, that the proceeding glories would be seasons of darkness and struggle that only God could see me through.

I realised that my seasons with God were actually cyclical, just like a tree. Winter comes and its leaves die, and as the season changes, it comes alive, looking as beautiful as ever, just to die again. However, after each summer, the tree grows bigger, taller, and stronger. But just as the natural pruning process happens, pruning is essential in the lives of Christians for both spiritual growth and growth in character. When we look at the Word, we know that we should be connected to the Vine (Jesus Christ) in order for us to be fruitful. John 15:1–2 says, "I am the true vine, and My Father is the vinedresser. Every branch in Me that does not bear fruit He takes away; and every *branch* that bears fruit He prunes, that it may bear more fruit" (NKJV).

Pruning is a good thing, even though most of the time it does not feel nice and sometimes we might lose everything. Despite that, we have hope that when the summer comes around once again, our branches will be beautiful. When God is pruning our lives, it is evident that we have been bearing fruit. If not, He would have totally disconnected us. Pruning is evidence of His love and confirmation that we are His children because God only disciplines those He loves (Heb. 12:6). Like a loving father, He cuts off the things that we may be in love with but that nonetheless hinder the relationship and spiritual growth necessary to our walk and our call with God.

During the last season of my life, I realised the greatest storms do the deepest work, and unlike trees, there is a struggle. Our sinful nature is struggling against us. Our flesh doesn't want to die but to live. The flesh does all it can, not only to control our being but to preserve itself. Yet without this death to self, new growth is impossible. The winters in our lives can be so bleak at times that we don't only wish we could die, but we actually believe we are dying. The pain, the trauma, and the heartaches during this time are inexplicable and at times so unbearable. I remember while I was going through the drama and trauma of my divorce, my parents went on holiday and invited three single ladies to come with them, including me (how nice). We had all been waiting for the court date so the drama could come to an end, so this holiday was intended to be a celebratory holiday.

The case was postponed, and it seemed like my life was hanging by a string. I was lifeless. I couldn't even focus to read. I would lay outside in the sun, numb, listening to a sermon on my iPod and wishing all the trauma and tragedy would end. As I lay there with the lovely sea hitting the rocks and the sun beaming down, my sweet comforter, the Holy Spirit, began to speak. He said, "Ruth, look in the sky; can't you see the sun of a new day and the moon of an old day? They are in the sky at the same time. You have to learn to deal with two seasons of life at the same time. Patiently wait for the moon, representing the dark season of your past, to no longer be seen and the sun to be at the highest point."

Oh what a joy and a comfort for the Holy Spirit to calm our storms and quiet the waves that bring anxiety into our hearts. I remember as an inner city child that I used to draw one picture of the sun with Mum, Dad, and the dog in it and a separate picture of the moon and the stars. I felt like this moment was the first time I had seen them in the sky together, and as I lay there, I watched the moon of yesterday pass and the sun come to the highest point. It was then I knew that my troubles would pass.

We all, when going through the pruning stage, have to learn how to manage the dying, dark seasons of our lives (the moon) while entering the glorious, sunny seasons of our lives (the day). From my experience, the night seasons in life are actually where transformation takes place—just like a butterfly in a cocoon who struggles to get out while all the time strengthening its wings. As we struggle out of our night seasons, we develop spiritual wings and character necessary for the season ahead.

Many things die in the night season. I believe part of me died when I was going through my divorce. I was empty and numb, and I couldn't see. I had lost my vision. But as the Son, Jesus Christ, began to rise in a new day, His light was able to shine through every broken area, making my life more beautiful than before. Because God's strength is made perfect in weakness and I truly had nothing left, I gained everything through Him. Second Corinthians 12:9 states, "And He said to me, 'My grace is sufficient for you, for My strength is made perfect in weakness.' Therefore most gladly I will rather boast in my infirmities, that the power of Christ may rest upon me" (NKJV).

God is so loving and gracious, even when we are wrong and make mistakes that would cause us to run and hide like Adam did. He seeks us out and still longs to love us. He knows us more than we know ourselves. In the words of David in Psalm 139:13–16:

"For You formed my inward parts; You covered me in my mother's womb. I will praise You, for I am fearfully and wonderfully made; Marvellous are Your works, And that my soul knows very well. My frame was not hidden from You, When I was made in secret, and skillfully wrought in the lowest parts of the earth. Your eyes saw my substance, being yet unformed. And in Your book they all were written, The days fashioned for me, When as yet there were none of them."

God knows us better than we know ourselves. Don't worry and go into condemnation. Just get back up and run to the Father. His arms are there, lovingly yearning and anticipating your return. He makes all things new, and He will clothe you and wash you, and you will not remember the pain of yesterday. What a mighty God! If He can save me, He can save you too. We can do all things as we lean on Him and His strength, to do in us and through us everything that is required.

During my dark season, the only thing stopping me from suicide was salvation and eternal damnation. If neither of these things existed, I would have ended my life. I thank God for His grace and my parents, who held me up at an expensive cost to themselves. I can remember times that I wish the ground would swallow me up. I went through things that broke me down to nothing and back into the arms of my Saviour. But I count it all joy. I truly do, because in the end, it is all for His glory. James1:2–4 says, "My brethren, count it all joy when you fall into various trials, knowing that the testing of your faith produces patience. But let patience have its perfect work, that you may be perfect and complete, lacking nothing" (NKJV).

There are some things of the world that are so deeply rooted that the process of taking them out is distressing, yet its eternal value is priceless. This is supported in Hebrews 12:5–6, where we are encouraged about God's discipline: "My son, do not despise the chastening of the Lord, Nor be discouraged when you are rebuked by Him; For whom the Lord loves He chastens, And scourges every son whom He receives."

CHAPTER FOUR

Fleeing the World

The pursuit into a deeper intimacy with God involves overcoming so many obstacles. First, we must truly say good-bye to the world. We have to examine every area of our lives to ensure that we are totally surrendered to God—that we have made Him Lord in every one of those areas and that we are not living for our own agendas. If we identify things we are struggling to give up or if we discover that there are idols in our lives, then this is a good time to cry out to God for help. Our instinct, like Adam, is to hide, but our help is in God, so we need to do the opposite and run to Him, crying for Him to change the areas of our lives that are keeping us bound to the things of the world. We have to remember God's Word that says, "If we confess our sins, he is faithful and just and will forgive us our sins and purify us from all unrighteousness" (1 John 1:9 NKJV). We also need to know that God's grace and mercy are there when we fall in our pursuit to look like Christ through the empowerment of the Holy Spirit.

Detachment from the World

Once we have detached ourselves from the world, we will notice that some of the world is still in us. We are now required to actively work with the Holy Spirit to remove the habits and behaviours of the flesh that keep us connected to the world. Just like we did in examining our lives, we need to do an inventory, asking the Holy Spirit to identify things to us that are hindering our walk. As He reveals it to us, we must take it back to Him, praying earnestly—and even fasting—for Him to change and transform us. This prayer has to be coupled with the practicing of righteousness as 2 Timothy 2:22 says, "Flee also youthful lusts; but pursue righteousness, faith, love, peace with those who call on the Lord out of a pure heart." (NKJV).

There must be a renewing of our minds (Rom. 12:2). We must re-educate ourselves on the things of God with a determination and active participation throughout our lives—taking off the old and embracing the new. This is done through reading the Word of God and learning about men and women of faith who have successfully grown in intimacy with God. We have to leave the old behaviours and habits behind that keep us bound and connected to the things of the world. Like any other habit, this will take time and active practice to achieve. But we have the Holy Spirit, who will empower us in answer to our prayer for change.

Leaving the world's culture, mind-set, and system is one thing, entering God's kingdom is another. This is also evident in the story of the sower who sowed seeds into the ground, but the love of the world and the cares of this world choked out their fruit. These people received and accepted the Word of God joyfully. They have left the world, forsaken their unbelief, and confessed that Jesus is Lord. Like the Israelites, they left Egypt, they danced, they sang, they encountered God, and they testified of His glory and power. They made a commitment and even joined the local church. They loved Christ. But the Word says that the cares of the world, the deceitfulness of riches, choked this out. In Matthew 13:22 it states, "Now he who received seed among the thorns is he who hears the word, and the cares of this world and the deceitfulness of riches choke the word and he becomes unfruitful" (NKJV).

The Thorn of My Flesh

The Word of God is sown into our hearts, and our hearts have thorns. These thorns are things of the flesh, things of the world, that will draw us out of the will of God to follow instead the desires and dictates of our carnal nature. When looking at plants, thorns and plants actually grow up together, meaning the Word is planted into the person's heart, and while this person actively believes, at the same time the thorn in his or her flesh is also growing at the same rate. These thorns choke out true spiritual growth, not allowing it to mature in the things of the Spirit or become fruitful. These thorns stunt spiritual growth, causing the Christian not to bear any fruit.

Paul experienced this thorn in the flesh. How did Paul deal with the thorn in his flesh? Studying 2 Corinthians 12:7–10, it says:

> *And lest I should be exalted above measure by the abundance of the revelations, a thorn in the flesh was given to me, a messenger of Satan to buffet me, lest I be exalted above measure. Concerning this thing I pleaded with the Lord three times that it might*

depart from me. And He said to me, "My grace is sufficient for you, for my strength is made perfect in weakness." Therefore most gladly I will rather boast in my infirmities, that the power of Christ may rest upon me. Therefore I take pleasure in infirmities, in reproaches, in needs, in persecutions, in distresses, for Christ's sake. For when I am weak, then I am strong.

As Paul was pressing into the things of God, a fleshly thorn was also evident in his side. This thorn was given to humble him so that he didn't boast of his great insights and revelations. A thorn is described in the dictionary as a stiff, sharp, pointed, woody projection, a source of discomfort, an irritation or obstacle, a bodily annoyance or disability. We need to look at this in terms of spiritual annoyance—something that would bring discomfort in Paul's spirit and thereby keep him humble, even broken.

If I analyse my spiritual life and the things I believe God requires of me personally, I can identify several things that cause me annoyance to my spiritual growth and walk. All these things are part of my carnal nature, and their purpose is to keep me down and to keep me grounded in the things of the world. One of them is gluttony or just not being obedient to my call to fast consistently. This is a major obstacle for me. I try sometimes and just fall flat on my face. Other times I'm doing well, but then I eat a piece of cake and totally mess up. The annoying thing is that once my diet goes wrong, it imbalances everything else in my life.

Another area I struggle in is when I can see that I am ready for spiritual lift-off, but then I get distracted by opening one door or another through not guarding my heart, and then I'm back down to earth again, hating myself for being a mess. I then wonder if I will ever be able to stay off the ground long enough to grow into maturity and to grow in the things of the spirit. As I sit and analyse, I see the pattern of my life before me. The more I desire God, the more mess is revealed. I feel like I'm in a hot air balloon, and in order to go into the sky, I have to offload every sin that hinders and every weight (Heb. 12:1).

God makes every area of weakness an area where we can be totally dependent on Him. Paul described his thorn in the flesh as a demon or messenger of satan, something to harass him and keep him humble so he would not become proud and feel like he was superior to others. He requested three times for the thorn to be removed from him. But the Lord said, "My grace is sufficient for you, for my power is made perfect in weakness." This means that His holy influence and power was strength enough for Paul. This means that His anointing and miracles were perfected in his inability, lack, and weakness. Where there is a need, a want, an inability to do something, then there is God's holy influence, power, and anointing to help us overcome. As we cry out and call upon Him, He will deliver us. God's power is made perfect in our inability.

So the annoying thorn is actually an opportunity. It is a reason to rejoice, a reason to celebrate and give praise. It allows us to humbly present ourselves before God, knowing our inability to transform anything by ourselves. This is where God's power can be seen through all the broken areas of our lives as we surrender and lean on Him to transform us into the image of Christ. He is always so gracious and faithful, waiting for us to come to Him, even when we fall a million times in one area. We must just realise that our change is reliant on our dependency and confidence in God. The more we attempt to overcome things of the flesh in our power, the more we will fall and the more powerless we feel. This is good because God is teaching us that we cannot change ourselves. Every time we fail, we come to believe the change we want is impossible, but "with God all things are possible" (Matt. 19:26 NKJV). So we must run to Him because what God requires from us as Christians is something only He can do. Only His power through the Holy Spirit can change us.

While we are taking off old habits and the things of the world, we must at the same time replace these things by putting on Christ in exactly the same way. This transformation is not something we can gain of ourselves through work, but it is achieved as we come to Christ in intimacy. We are transformed as he gives us the grace to practice righteousness. As we go through this life-changing process, we grow in intimacy with God.

Pursuing Intimacy with God Means Pursuing Holiness

Getting closer to God requires us to become holy like He is holy. I passionately believe we need more holiness teaching and preaching in our churches. When you go back to our Christian heritage of Charles Spurgeon, John Wesley, William Law, J. C. Ryle, and even more recently Leonard Ravenhill, you can see that these men knew God and lived a life crucifying the flesh in order to be able to pursue the holiness that can only be released by earnestly seeking God in heartfelt repentance for complete change.

This has eternal implications and is serious business. It is truly something we would not want to take lightly. Psalm 15 says:

Lord, who may abide in Your tabernacle? Who may dwell in Your holy hill? He who walks uprightly, And works righteous-

ness, And speaks the truth in his heart; He who does not back-bite with his tongue, Nor does evil to his neighbour, Nor does he take up a reproach against his friend; In whose eyes a vile person is despised, But he honours those who fear the Lord; He who swears to his own hurt and does not change; He who does not put out his money at usury, Nor does he take a bribe against the innocent. He who does these things shall never be moved. (NKJV)

One of the key themes running through this section of the book is that pursuing intimacy with God means pursuing holiness. The Word of God says that without holiness, no man can see God (Heb. 12:14). This holiness needs to be practically seen in the life of the believer.

We see in Psalm 15 a clear description of one who wants to dwell or abide in God's presence. The Psalm looks at the disposition and the character of those who will be able to enter into His presence, and these characteristics are important for us to look at as we also try to enter an intimate relationship with God. The questions posed in the first verse, "Lord, who may abide in Your tabernacle? Who may dwell in Your holy hill?" shows us who will come into God's presence and who will stay with Him both here on earth and in heaven. The Psalm is looking at God's perspective, what He wants, because it is necessary.

Entering God's presence is not just guaranteed to anyone. We may feel that it is enough to have gone to church for twenty years as a professing Christian. We may even believe that saying a prayer and letting God into his or her heart without any change in heart entitles us to encounter God's presence here and in eternity. To enable us to really understand God's viewpoint, we must ask God some important questions. We must ask what does God require of us as believers? What are the attributes of one who will be able to get close to God? The rest of the Psalm brings the answer. These questions are asked by the souls that are unsatisfied and want to encounter and be with God both now and in heaven.

Walks Uprightly

We all know that in order for us to even start walking, we need a destination or a goal. Based on that destination, we order our steps and our lives in a way that gets us to the location unhindered. In our walk as Christians, this looks at our journey along the path of faith as we align ourselves with the Word of God. If we are to enter His presence and grow into intimacy, God requires that we live in a manner that is upright and righteous, befitting one who professes the faith. Genesis 17:1 says, "Walk before me and be thou perfect" (KJV). We must walk every day with a conscious reality of God watching us and live in a manner that is truly pleasing to Him, according to His Word. A very practical way to keep God ever before us is to meditate and ponder on the Scriptures and what is required. This will enable us to check our every action according to the Word of God.

Works Righteousness

This looks at our works in our daily living, not merely works of charity but also the interactions with people at work or within our business—how we conduct ourselves in the workplace and how we conduct ourselves in our relationship with God. God expects our works, whether at home, in the workplace, or in the church, to be done in righteousness. This requires us to be more watchful of how we conduct ourselves so that we can be more deliberate in how we react and ensure that the things we do bring glory to God and contribute to our further walk into His presence. God requires us to do all our dealings according to the instructions given in His Word, working in the way of the commandments and instruction given for holy living within the Scriptures.

Speaks the Truth in His Heart

The way we speak is very important to God, and God requires us to speak the truth to others and to Him as it is in our hearts. Nevertheless, when we go deeper into this Psalm, we will see that God requires us to speak uprightly and not to slander or sin with our mouths. Proverbs 18:21 states, "Death and life are in the power of the tongue" (NKJV). We are also told to edify others with our speech. If we daily meditate and fill ourselves with the wisdom and teaching in God's Word along with the wisdom from the lives of holy men and women of God down through the ages, we will fill our hearts and minds with truth. This truth will be able to overflow into our discussions with others. If we are really walking in the manner required by God, we should be full of Christ and full of His Word. This will overflow in everything we do in word, actions, and motives.

As we continue to read Psalm 15, we can see more and more of the characteristics required for us to walk with God. God requires us to live holy lives in word and action. The Bible commands us to be holy because He is holy (1 Peter 1:16). God does not expect us to believe that Jesus died on the cross to free us from sin without also believing that it is possible for us to actively live out God's requirement through the power of the Holy Spirit.

In the same way that Psalm 15 asks about who may abide and dwell with God, Psalm 24 speaks of ascending into the hill of the Lord and standing in His holy place. In both of these Psalms, Matthew Henry's commentary sees this as asking, "Who shall go to heaven hereafter, and as an earnest of that, shall have communion with God in holy ordinances now?"

> *Who may ascend into the hill of the Lord? Or who may stand in His holy place? He who has clean hands and a pure heart, Who has not lifted up his soul to an idol, Nor sworn deceitfully. He shall receive blessing from the Lord, And righteousness from the God of his salvation. This is Jacob, the generation of those who seek Him, Who seek Your face. Selah. (Ps. 24:3–6 NKJV)*

Clean Hands

A clean hand deals with the outward expression of how we live our lives. It looks at what a person says and does. Do people live in a way that is holy and acceptable to God, or are they after the dictates or culture of the world and the desires of their fleshy nature? They are to live seeking the way of the Spirit and conduct themselves in a manner that is pleasing to God and a blessing to man. They must become eternally minded.

Clean hands mean that we must not do anything in action or speech to hinder others, resulting in their disconnection from God. This could include avoiding financial discrepancies and living above reproach in all that we do.

Pure Heart

A pure heart looks at the inward expression of how we live before God. It looks at our thoughts and desires and the foundation of our daily lives. There are many believers who would say they are morally sound in action and deed and successfully live in a manner that harms no one. However, there are some signs that are both overlooked and minimised by categorising sin. This includes the sins of the heart and mind, which often betray us in our speech. This includes self-righteousness, gossiping, envy, slander, worldliness, and unforgiveness. These things not only defile our hearts, but they also disconnect us from our eternal destination if they are not dealt with and overcome.

We must deal with both our inward life and outward action to truly pursue the path of holiness into God's presence. Even those with an outward show of holiness need to really examine their hearts and inward life and "rend their hearts," as the Word says, removing anything that would hinder our love with God or man.

Those who have clean hands and pure hearts are unable to live by the dictates of the flesh and will instead live with the Word of God as a light to their path. This protects them from having idols as they set their hearts, minds, and bodies to live after the will of

God. Their speech will also be free from deceit, just as David indicated in Psalm 39:1,

"I said, "I will guard my ways, lest I sin with my tongue; I will restrain my mouth with a muzzle, while the wicked are before me."(NKJV).

There is a clear requirement from God in this Scripture and also in Psalm 24 that we must be a people in pursuit of holiness. This must affect the way we live, speak, and walk daily and deal with people in general. We cannot adopt the behaviour of the world that is so aggressively promoted everywhere we go. We see it amongst work colleagues, on advertising posters, on TV, and in magazines.

Eunice Upright

Eunice Upright is known for her love of God. She tries to walk in a way that is pleasing to God. At all times she fails. Nevertheless with practice, those around her can see that she is progressing in the way of righteousness. Eunice spends most of her spare time studying the Bible and studying the life of Jesus and the words He spoke so she can align her life to God's purpose and will. She loves reading books that draw her into a closer relationship with God and often buys books about men and women of God that have gone before her.

She starts the day early at 5:00 a.m., before work and before her children get up so that she can spend time in the Word, in prayer, and in committing her day to God. She refrains from watching TV, secular films, and the media in order not to be conformed to this world. She wants to be single-minded in her pursuit of God. Once her day begins, she gets lunch ready for her children while she meditates on the Scriptures she studied that morning. She also prays in her heart and mind as she prepares and gets ready for work.

When Eunice is at work, she is very friendly, gentle, and quiet, always watching over her thoughts and words in order not to offend man or God. Her colleagues see her as a woman of few words but a very encouraging and wise person who shares her love of God in both word and deed. Occasionally she unknowingly stops guarding her heart, which causes her to stumble as she engages in carnal discussions around the vanities of this world. At times like this, Eunice cries out to God for forgiveness and the grace to do better. She often forgets how far she has progressed in overcoming trials, temptations, and sins in order to become one with God. Sometimes she gets discouraged when her flesh tries to sabotage her walk, yet this simply brings her down to her knees as she knows that where she is weak, God will show Himself to be strong.

Eunice's fellow believer and sister in Christ, Mary Mediocre, believes Eunice is taking her walk far too seriously. They often have conversations on how Eunice lives her life. Mary Mediocre just can't understand why she gets up so early to pray and why she would fast on a weekly basis. Mary argues that Eunice is unsociable, but Eunice gently explains that she refrains from worldly activities and outings that bring no blessing to her soul and are contradictory to God's Word. Mary is a bit confused as she isn't sufficiently familiar with her Bible or the verse in Psalm 34:13 that says, "Keep your tongue from evil, and your lips from speaking deceit." Mary's Bible study is limited to the Sunday morning preaching and the few words shared in fellowship.

Mary Mediocre

Mary loves church and wouldn't miss it for anything. If she doesn't attend, people know something has gone wrong. Mary is active in the prayer ministry and also helps out in the church café. She's been a Christian for fifteen years and tries her best to minster to those in need.

Once Mary gets home, her life is no different from the life of anyone else in the world. She watches all the soaps and reality shows until she falls asleep in front of the TV. She intended to just watch the TV for an hour, because she had planned on reading her Bible, but there just never seems to be enough time. So she goes to bed exhausted but makes time when the phone rings and one of her friends wants to give her the latest gossip on who just got divorced. She says all manner of things that she shouldn't, and through the conversation you hear, "Oh I shouldn't have said that! God forgive me." But there is no change in her conversation. Over the years, she has simply learned the skill of disguising gossiping and slander for sharing or "telling the truth."

She finally gets to bed almost at midnight. Laying down, she says two minutes of prayer before she falls asleep. Mary has been encouraged by Eunice to give her mornings to God, so her alarm is set for 6:30 a.m. She hears the alarm going off but turns it off and returns to sleep, convincing herself that God will understand. She finally gets up at 7:45 a.m., running around frantically to get ready and make the 8:30 train. She just makes it. She always carries a small Bible with her. But, time is running against her, so she pulls out her makeup bag and continues getting herself ready for the day ahead.

She gets to work and talks just like the world does, judging people, gossiping, and the only thing that defines her as being a Christian is the cross she wears around her neck. She puts in a travel claim for a trip she got for free and uses the office phone to make personal calls. Not convicted at all, she joins the girls to go to the local pub for a drink, joking about how Jesus turned water into wine. A bit tipsy, she gets in at 10:00 p.m. and listens to a message on the answering machine from Eunice, who had called to pray at a pre-arranged time with her. Mary had forgotten all about it. Totally tired, she gets ready for bed and falls asleep. This is Mary's life. She gets about fifteen minutes of prayer in a week, and ten of those minutes are in church.

Mary doesn't believe she needs to change the way she lives too much. She believes God's grace is sufficient and she is going to heaven just the way she is.

Heart Expression

The important thing to note in these two lives is not the outward expression of their walks. Everyone is at a different stage in their lives. In fact, when I met God, I was still drinking and smoking and very much filled with the things of the world. The key is the heart's desire to press forward into God for change. We see that

Eunice is seeking and Mary isn't. This is the fundamental difference between them.

One person may still be living in sin but may be hungering and thirsting after God, pursuing Him with love, and being transformed in the process. As they seek God, worldly habits drop off and change is evident. Even though this is a process and could take a lifetime, the closer we get to God, the more we are transformed into His image. In the same way, the less we seek and desire God, the more carnal and worldly we will become.

Not What You Say

"But be doers of the word, and not hearers only, deceiving yourselves. For if anyone is a hearer of the word and not a doer, he is like a man observing his natural face in a mirror; for he observes himself, goes away, and immediately forgets what kind of man he was. But he who looks into the perfect law of liberty and continues in it, and is not a forgetful hearer but a doer of the work, this one will be blessed in what he does." (James 1:22–25)

Eunice's pursuit of God comes from a hunger and thirst for God. She seeks to please God with every area of her life. She doesn't want to do anything in word or deed that would offend God or would hinder her from developing or growing in the things of the Spirit. She has centred her life on Christ, waking early just like Christ to seek God in prayer. She doesn't just hear the Word, but she puts value on the Word and endeavours to live and do according to the Word of God.

Mary is such a good example of someone professing to be saved but the change sadly is not evident in any way within her life. Believing in Christ is a good starting point. However, God does not want us to be simply hearers of the Word but doers. Belief in Christ is not only shown in words but can be seen in the way we live our lives. If Mary truly believed everything Jesus said in the New Testament, surely she would bring the things she was struggling with to the throne of grace, seeking God's empowerment for change. She would have read about denying herself and taking up her cross. This could mean simply changing the way she lives, adjusting her time, or relinquishing some negative worldly relationships that are leading her out of the will of God.

However, we can't make this assessment based solely on how a person lives. There are many who have their lives in perfect order, yet their hearts are so far from God. Their actions become very pharisaic because they have worked at changing the outward display of righteousness without changing the position of their hearts. To truly seek God with everything means we desire to please God and seek God and not please or seek self-gratification or living life according to desires and dictates of the flesh.

Lukewarmness

The frightening thing about Mary's way of life is the self-deception. She believes she is a Christian and is going to heaven, even though it is evident by her life that she is ignoring the things of the Spirit. The Word tells us that love of the world is enmity with God

(James 4:4). Even though she professes Christ with her lips, her life is evidence of someone who isn't living for Christ. She is living for herself, fulfilling any desire and lust she has while practicing no righteousness or self-control in her life. Mary will engage in a variety of worldly discourses as she isn't watchful or looking at her actions in the light of Scripture to discern if her life is one suited to the Christianity she professes.

Mary's life has no conviction, no pressing towards or fighting towards the goal. She has no Christian goal, in fact, except that of doing service for others within her church. This is so unlike Eunice, who is cultivating the oil required to keep her light burning for Christ's return.

Mary has the Word and is a professing Christian, but she is not investing in the oil of the Holy Spirit through intimacy. Just like the five virgins who did not invest in getting oil, she will not be ready at Christ's return—regardless of how much she has deceived herself into believing that she will be (Matt. 25:1–13). As the Word says, we reap what we sow (Gal. 6:7–9). If we sow things into the flesh then we reap things of the flesh.

Mary will hardly feel any opposition in her Christian walk since she is conformed to the world and is flowing in the direction of the world—unlike Eunice, who wrestles daily to win spiritual battles and often feels defeated as she swims against the current and waves of the world and the desires of the flesh. She does this in order to win the prize of eternal life and her desire to be with God.

The Sunday service could act as an idol for Mary since she doesn't have any other form of devotion, and so her Christianity is simply determined by church dependency without any effort to nurture a personal relationship with Christ. Unfortunately, this dependency is further developed and enriched by the fellowship of others during the Sunday service. It is an even greater concern to see Mary in the prayer ministry team when she doesn't cultivate a personal relationship with God in her secret place of prayer. Mary looks more interested in the external expression of Christianity in comparison to a changed heart and a transformed mind, both of which God requires. In E. M. Bounds' book on prayer,[16] he says that we need the whole man to pray:

"It takes whole-hearted men to keep God's commandments and it demands the same sort of man to seek God…Just as it requires a whole heart given to God to gladly and fully obey God's commandments, so it takes a whole heart to do effectual praying. Be-

---

[16] E. M. Bounds, *The Complete Works of E. M. Bounds on Prayer* (Grand Rapids, MI: Baker Books, 2008).

cause it requires the whole man to pray, praying is no easy task. Praying is far more than simply bending the knee and saying a few words by rote.

> Tis not enough to bend the knee,
> And words of prayer to say;
> The heart must with the lips agree,
> Or else we do not pray.[17]

When looking at Mary's life in light of E. M. Bounds' words, we see that despite her token prayers, her life is in direct opposition to the prayers she offers. She lives a life of lukewarmness, with no hunger and thirst towards God. E. M. Bounds expounds on the fact that a person's prayer is effectual when his or her life is totally devoted to God. Furthermore, he explains that true effectual prayer bears fruits of consecration, and you cannot pray effectually without consecration. Also consecration cannot be gained without prayer. In the words of E. M. Bounds:

> Consecration is not so much the setting one's self apart from sinful things and wicked ends, but rather it is the separation from the worldly, secular and even legitimate things, if they come into conflict with God's plans, to holy uses. It is the devoting of all we

---

[17] Ibid., 83–84.

have to God for His own specific use. It is separation from things questionable, or even legitimate, when the choice is to be made between the things of this life and the claims of God ...Consecration being the intelligent, voluntary act of the believer, this act is the direct result of praying. No prayer-less man ever conceives the idea of a full consecration. It leads nowhere else. In fact, a life of prayer is satisfied with nothing else but an entire dedication of one's self to God. Consecration recognises fully, God's ownership of us. It cheerfully assents to the truth set forth by Paul: Ye are not your own. "For ye are bought with a price. Therefore, glorify God in your body and spirit, which are God's."[18]

Mary is far from consecration or even desiring a life of holiness that will lead to a closer relationship with God. She has been deceived into believing that her walk will get her to heaven. She hasn't been challenged about her walk with God and has been deluded that this way of living gives any glory to God. She rejoices as God answers her many prayers for others, forgetting the ministers who stated to Christ when refused entry into the kingdom, "Have we not ... cast out demons in Your name?" (Matt. 7:22 NKJV).

---

[18] Ibid., 119.

Mary has no spiritual goals in developing her heart towards the things of God. Thus all the terms in the Bible about practicing righteousness are alien to her. To add insult to injury, she has now become a hindrance to others seeking Christ, as they see her lukewarm walk where everything is permissible.

Outwardly, and even amongst her Christian friends, Mary seems to be heavenly minded. This is further reinforced by the good deeds she does in church and for the people she helps. She is always there for people in their time of need, and from a worldly sense, she is always helpful and making an outward difference in the lives of others. She is ever busy running a Christian women's group who socialise and meet regularly to fellowship. Nevertheless, I would truly question the spiritual impact this will make led by someone who is carnally minded and simply shares what she has spiritually eaten through the week: TV, gossip, slander, and backbiting.

You are what you eat. If you fill yourself with worldly counsel, then you will be living unconsciously under the influence and direction of the world as this will be the dominant input in your life. Mary cannot expect to sow in the flesh and reap of the Spirit. Before we can reap of the things of the Spirit, we have to first invest in the things of the Spirit. You need to be like Eunice, reading the Word, searching, hungering, and thirsting for God with your whole life and communing with Him in prayer.

Mary's life is filled and dominated with so many worldly things that the energy to truly invest in the things of the Spirit isn't there. She has no desire to do so since she is already full and satisfied as she lives her life to the fullest now. However, she is diligent in even the smallest things of her life, such as getting to work on time, but she doesn't invest in feeding or developing her spiritual man to enable her to communion with God now and in the end.

Today we live in a generation of busyness and everything is fast—fast food, fast cars, and fast communication. Being busy has robbed many Christians of the spiritual growth and maturity needed to be effective for the kingdom of God. There always seems to be time for everything else, time to do the essentials and the things believed to be important to us. But as always, just like the life of Mary, God gets the short straw, and very often our priorities don't include God. Many lose their first love through the deception of busyness—often too busy doing things that in the end will simply not count.

I remember a family discussion about seeing an old friend. My dad said he hadn't been able to see this friend because his friend was always too busy.

My mum said something that will never leave me. She said that people make time for people who are important to them—even when they are busy. This runs true with our relationship with God. If we had any value for our relationship with Him, we would have time and make time for Him. If we truly believe that our righteousness is not based on our self but dependant on God, we will be at His feet daily, seeking Him to empower us to live in this world undefiled through the power of the Holy Spirit.

Our actions give us a clue as to who we are dependent upon. If we are not dependent on God, then we are dependent on self. And the fruit of self is reliance on the things of the world. Our attitude to the things of God is evidence of our independence from God. Mary, judging herself against the standards of the world, may see herself as having clean hands and pure heart; after all, she hasn't murdered anyone. Yet according to God's Word, there are many warnings about her way of living, including Revelation 3:15–16, which states, "I know your works, that you are neither cold nor hot. I could wish you were cold or hot. So then, because you are lukewarm, and neither cold nor hot, I will vomit you out of My mouth."

What a daunting thought to be cut off from God because of being lukewarm and having a laid-back approach to God while paying no regard to our spiritual condition to the extent of being blinded and deceived. When we consider how diligent we are in worldly affairs, the sowing and reaping principle is evident in every area of our lives. For example, if we plant an apple tree, no one expects that it will bring forth pears. If you live life eating junk food and getting no exercise, everyone knows that this will have adverse effect on your health. It can cause a heart attack. The sowing and reaping principle is so clear that surely we would know that what dominates our lives is evidence of whether we are sowing to the things of the Spirit or flesh. We can see our condition—and even at times identify it for what it is—yet the cares of this world and the deceitfulness of riches keeps us bound, unable to invest in the spiritual essentials that lead to the narrow path and into eternal life.

More seriously there are those of us who know something is wrong. We can sense it, yet because of sheer laziness and counting the cost of being a disciple, we are not willing to go and follow Christ and carry our cross. We prefer the broad way of comfort, entertainment, and self-indulgence that leads to eternal punishment. So even though we engage in all the religious activities available, we are not reliant on Him and do not know Him. We may have head knowledge gained through the years of attending church, but the knowledge of God requires an experiential relationship where we are dependent and humble and seek to please Him with every area of our lives. Walking in holiness, we must be a living sacrifice. Romans 12:1–2 says,

> "I beseech you therefore, brethren, by the mercies of God, that you present your bodies as a living sacrifice, holy, acceptable to God, which is your reasonable service. And do not be conformed to this world, but be transformed by the renewing of your mind, that you may prove what is that good and acceptable and perfect will of God."

CHAPTER FIVE

On Your Mark, Get Set

"If anyone comes to Me and does not hate his father and mother, wife and children, brothers and sisters, yes, and his own life also, he cannot be My disciple. And whoever does not bear his cross and come after Me cannot be My disciple. For which of you, intending to build a tower, does not sit down first and count the cost, whether he has enough to finish it—lest, after he has laid the foundation, and is not able to finish, all who see it begin to mock him, saying, 'This man began to build and was not able to finish'? Or what king, going to make war against another king, does not sit down first and consider whether he is able with ten thousand to meet him who comes against him with twenty thousand? Or else, while the other is still a great way off, he sends a delegation and asks conditions of peace. So

likewise, whoever of you does not forsake all that he has cannot be My disciple. (Luke 14:26–33 NKJV)

The above words spoken by Jesus show us the importance of being able to count the cost of being His disciple. We have to understand what it is that God requires on the narrow path, and if we are willing to take His invitation to come, then we must deny ourselves and take up our cross and follow Him (Matt. 16:24). This commitment will require some effort and practical working out on our part. We must sit back and count the cost of what is required of us. Everyone's cross is different on this narrow path. Some people may be aware of it, and most stumble under it as they continue on their journey walking in line with God's Word. One cross that is common to all Christians is the Christian disciplines to flee the world (James 4:4, John 2:15), pursue holiness (1 Peter 1:14–16, Heb. 12:14, Matt. 5:8, Eph. 1:4), practice righteousness (1 Tim. 4:7, Heb. 5:14), and take off the old man and put on Christ (Eph. 4:17–24) as we grow in maturity and towards the full stature of Christ (Eph. 4:13). This requires discipline and perseverance as it is in direct opposition to the things of this world and its culture.

In this section, we will be looking at what it means to: (1) flee the world, (2) pursue holiness and practice righteousness, (3) and take off the old man and put on Christ as we grow in maturity and grow towards the (4) full stature of Christ. When growing up as children, most of us can't wait to be teenagers, and as teenagers, we cannot wait to be adults. However, as we grow older, we realise that with the newfound freedom comes responsibility. In the same way, there are childish and immature ways that are appropriate for those who are growing into spiritual maturity. Just as in the physical, as we develop habits in order to grow in spiritual maturity, it requires that we develop spiritual disciplines that help us grow in the things of the Spirit.

As we go on our personal journeys of pursuit, it is important that we actually know what it means to do the above and how it is implemented into everyday life. First, before we even try to start this process, there has to be a hunger and thirst to seek after God and how to please God. No one in pursuit of God can take one step unless there is a deep desire—a yearning—that rises up within our souls despite the sins, storms, and many temptations we have while living on this earth. There must be a desire not to settle for the status quo but a searching for God and His will, as if looking for treasure. Only this hunger and thirst can wake up the carnal soul to pursue the deeper things of God and to overcome and win the battle.

The Word of God

The Bible is no longer an opened book. People in this generation are now living Christian lives without the Word of God. If being led by the Spirit is divorced from the Bible, then all you have is error and something that is not Christianity at all. Christianity is based on the Word of God, which never changes. The Word does the work of sanctification and purification, and without it, we will remain dead in our sins and disconnected from true salvation.

We must strive to get our lives back in line with the written Word of God. When we want to go somewhere, we use a map or a navigation system to help us locate our destination. Even when using appliances like washing machines and ovens, instruction manuals are given to aid us in our use of them.

I recall when my mum wanted to change the clock on our new oven. I was convinced I could change it without a manual. How wrong I was, thinking if I just pressed the buttons in different sequences, I would be able to change it. However, this was not the case, and my efforts were in vain. My mum, after watching in amusement, pulled out the instruction manual and changed the clock with ease. God has given us the instruction manual for our lives—the Bible, the living Word of God that has the power to transform lives. The Bible must be our sole authority, and we must refrain from assumptions and presumptions and stand on God's Word as the only definite and sovereign rule under which we live every aspect of our lives.

We must not waste time like I did trying to make the oven work without looking at the instructions. We cannot guess God's will and purpose, and we have no real need to because His Word is clearly there. When we try to work God's will out with our carnal minds, we are actually prone to error as "the heart of man is desperately wicked."(Jeremiah 17:9) We will minimise God's sovereignty as we try to comprehend His ways with worldly and carnal ideas. God's Word says His ways are higher than our ways.

Fleeing the world means just that—leaving behind everything to do with our old, worldly way of life to embrace the way and life of the Spirit. It would be leaving the culture of the world with all its greed and vanity. It means leaving everything that is in direct and even indirect opposition to the Word of God.

In a war, we usually see people fleeing an active combat zone. They hardly carry anything because of the hasty manner in which they left. To flee indicates running or escaping from impending danger. This is exactly what we must do as the world will defile anyone who aims to pursue God. The world is dangerous to the spiritual health and growth of all believers. The world has been developed to keep people grounded and hell-bound by offering values and ideas that are appealing to the flesh and the carnal soul, yet have the ability to paralyse their victims, hastening them on to a spiritual death.

The Bible speaks about renewing our minds. If we remain connected to the world or even remain on the fence where we profess Christ, while indulging in every fantasy that our flesh brings to mind; then we will be wasting our time and will not be making any progress. It would be like a person trying to lose weight by exercising, yet he or she eats so much that it makes their efforts pointless and losing weight impossible. This will continue until this person makes a decision to reduce or even stop their excess intake of wrong foods. Only then will they see a change.

Worldliness

When looking at worldliness, it is necessary that we don't look simply at the fruits of our daily activity and life in an attempt to change behaviour. We must consider the root of the problem. Worldliness is a position and attitude of the heart. If we simply focus on the external, we are merely dealing with the weeds, which will only return after a time. The issue is one of the heart. The Pharisees in the Bible attempted to make the outside of the cup clean, but Jesus said in Matthew 23:25–26, "Woe to you, scribes and Pharisees, hypocrites! For you cleanse the outside of the cup and dish, but inside they are full of extortion and self-indulgence. Blind Pharisee, first cleanse the inside of the cup and dish, that the outside of them may be clean also" (NKJV).

We see in James 4:4 that friendship with the world means hatred towards God and vice-versa. This is the key description of worldliness. It loves the world, and this plays out in the lives of worldly people, who instead of seeking what satisfies and makes God happy are pleasure seekers, seeking things that excite and give life to the flesh. They daily seek the sensual, carnal, and worldly pleasures, looking for things that are self-fulfilling and pleasing to their flesh. People with worldly minds may even be professing Christians. Nevertheless, they put the love of pleasure, comfort, and things of this world as their first priority, and this is evident in their actions, speech, way of life, and decisions.

As we pursue God and grow into deeper intimacy with Him by doing His will and desiring Him, the worldliness begins to fall away because as the Word says, we cannot love the world and love God at the same time. Fleeing the world is simply running into the arms of a loving God, seeking Him first, and seeking to obey His Word and ways. His Word will convict and sanctify us as we draw closer to Him. So by loving God and seeking Him with all our hearts, we disconnect from the love of the world, and instead, the truth of seeking Him will be evident in our lives through our fruits and the decisions and choices we make.

In second Timothy 2:22, *Flee* is a word used in to describe running away from youthful lusts. This means to run for your life and don't look back—just as those who are under attack must flee before the battle overtakes their homes and destroys them all. In the same way, we must run for our lives and flee lusts, the things of the world, and things that ultimately determine our eternal destination.

I believe we are living in a generation where hell and heaven, judgement, and eternity are fossils that have been truly put to one side and not spoken about. There is no urgency to get ready to meet Jesus. It is no longer the desire of the saints to press into righteousness. This generation of Christians is too focused on earthly, carnal, and shallow things. The world's things are temporarily satisfying, but they leave our spirits feeble and unprepared for the coming of our Saviour.

Yes, we believe. Yes, we said a prayer and asked God into our hearts. Yes, we attend Sunday services when we can. Yet much is lacking in this form of worship. As there is no Spirit and definitely no truth in this form of Christianity, the inner man dies of starvation. There is no longer talk of the holy God who requires a holy people, let alone training and support toward the practice of righteousness

When I was growing up in church, the term 'leaving the world' meant just that! While reverence and honour were rightly placed on the Word of God, I nevertheless witnessed believers who had lost their first love. If our love for God and our love for His Word have become separated, then we have, or we will become lukewarm in our faith. It now appears we have thrown the baby of 'pursuing righteousness' out with the bath water of 'legalism.' We must stand on the fact that God's Word never changes even though modern-day believers appeared to have not merely removed the signpost but have gone to great lengths to replace it. But in doing so, the consequences of disobedience still remain.

Yes, we must live in the world, but in doing so, we must break the influences that pull us further away from God. We must change from living according to the values of the world and replace them with the values as set out in His Word. Parents continually warn their children about bad influences in their lives. They say, "This child will get you in trouble," or "stop speaking to this person or that person." Why do we do that? We do it because we are in agreement with the Word of God, and it is this that tells us bad company corrupts good character (1 Cor. 15:33). We know this to be true, yet many of us refuse to accept that daily input from worldly friends and lukewarm Christians will result in the corruption of God's word.

This is always a sensitive and challenging subject, but as crazy as it sounds when we soak up the worldly enjoyment and advice, we enter into their silent hatred of God. In the guise of saving souls, we end up conforming to their way of living. So much so, that no one can tell the difference between them and us. This lame attempt to win them for Christ has now reinstated us back into the world we previously fled. Before long we once again become an enemy of the God we claim to worship on a Sunday.

The problem is that many of us in this situation know we are no longer growing spiritually; in fact, our walk with God has become a dull duty. Gone is the vibrant, passionate spirit we once had, all because we fail to realise that our associations are the root of the problem.

Now would be a good time to look into our lives. Yes God saved us, yet we are unwilling to give up our toys, pleasures, and worldly delights. This is why we are no longer growing and impacting His Kingdom. We have still maintained a greater sense of urgency and discipline for the things of this life and world and not a fraction of the same urgency and discipline for the things of God and the Spirit.

If we are unable to flee the worldly things that hold us, then we are unwilling to follow Christ. We deny Christ just because we choose our desires rather than obedience to His will. This is akin to having a house with holes in the roof, then wondering why we get wet when it rains. God has told many professing church going Christians to change things in their lives, leave friendships, and associations. Yet we have believed the lie of our flesh and deceived ourselves into thinking that everything is fine and that God couldn't be so hard. Have we read the scripture that describes God as a jealous God? Yes, He loves us, but He wants us all to Himself. In fact, the Bible says we were created to worship Him (Rev. 4:9–11). It's just that simple.

Pursue Holiness

James 2:26 says, "Faith without works is dead" (NKJV).

We are all aware that it is simply by the grace of God that we gain salvation and not by our works.

This is so because of the blood that Jesus shed for us. We cannot dispense with His holy requirement of being set apart as living sacrifices for His purpose. Yes, we are justified by faith and not by the works of the law. But we cannot use grace as a means to eradicate the work of the Holy Spirit in sanctification. God's requirement and call on us is to be holy as He is holy (1 Peter 1:16). This seems to be the core issue. The salvation we receive from God is not merely a salvation that is dead. God's Spirit is ever working in the lives of believers who are yielded to His purifying work, trying to bring them to the full stature of Christ.

The same faith that brought us into salvation is the faith that will cleanse us from all unrighteousness, being spotless and blameless for God's use. Don't think that in our practice of righteousness we gain "brownie points" and get to heaven that way. No, it's by grace we are saved, but as part of this salvation, God requires us to pursue righteousness and to be holy like He is holy.

"For we ourselves were also once foolish, disobedient, deceived, serving various lusts and pleasures, living in malice and envy, hateful and hating one another. But when the kindness and the love of God our Saviour toward man appeared, *not* by works of righteousness which we have done, but according to His mercy He saved us, through the washing of regeneration and renewing of the Holy Spirit, whom He poured out on us abundantly through Jesus Christ our Saviour, that having been justified by His grace we should become heirs according to the hope of eternal life. This is a faithful saying, and these things I want you to affirm constantly, that those who have believed in God should be careful to maintain good works. These things are good and profitable to men." (Titus 3:3–8 NKJV)

However, if a professing Christian comes to Christ by grace and yet lives a life contradictory to the faith he professes, this is not Christianity but merely lip service. God has laid this out in His Word, telling us what is acceptable and expected of those who are called by His name. The Holy Spirit is holy, and His work in the believer is the transforming of the unregenerate man into the likeness of God through sanctification. The error has developed because of a lack of basic biblical teachings on words like *sanctification*, which means the process of making a person holy and just. Twenty-first-century Christians have stopped at the justification by faith and starve their spiritual man through indulgence in activities not associated with our mothers and fathers of the faith.

Practising righteousness is simply the working out of one who is saved. The Christian who receives salvation dies to his flesh and gives his life to Christ to see how he could live in a manner pleasing to God. He does not try to gain salvation through the practice of works, but as a person who is saved, he seeks those things that are pleasing to his Master. Our pursuit of holiness and the likeness of God is a response to the love He showed us by dying on the cross. Because He gave us everything, there is an internal longing to surrender all and give Him everything in response to His love.

Many will read this book and will end up having an internal battle. This battle is because we love ourselves and the world more than we long for God. Our hearts betray us because of our reluctance to give God everything. This shows the value we truly place on His sacrifice. Yet still, there are some who will read this and desire even more to go deeper and deeper in surrender to Him, wanting to lay down their all for a treasure of great worth.

The true believer searches the Scripture and his life to find ways he can live that are pleasing to God. Just like David, these believers have a deep inner desire to live a life pleasing to God—no matter how many times they fall down and get back up. Even though this rising and falling is ever continuous in our lives and we wrestle with our flesh, we still cry out that we may know Him and be transformed into His image. The true believer, when searching the Scriptures, never sees God's commands as lofty, unattainable, or just simply words. But with childlike faith, he believes and asks God to release the grace needed to attain the godly attributes evident in Scripture. The holiness and character of God is beautifully displayed in Scripture by the requirements of those He calls out of the world. Sadly, if there isn't a yearning and delight in the holiness of God, and a willingness to press into the practice of righteousness, a pursuit of holiness, and a receiving and hearing of the Word without a sincere heart change and action, then this may well be evidence of a heart gone lukewarm or one who simply doesn't know God.

Many Christians lose their way because they may have pursued God fervently when they first believed, but they reduced their zeal and fervency to the level of those around them. They start to compare their walk to Christians who are no longer on the narrow path, which has only caused them to end up spiritually shipwrecked, with no evidence of the vibrant spirit they once had when they first believed. However, they have a form of godliness as they attend church and have an outward display of commitment to God, but their hearts are far from Him. They compare themselves with themselves, and this keeps them on the broad way, having calculated themselves in their own eyes to be morally okay…with just a few issues here and there. But, we shouldn't be looking at each other to measure our spiritual progress but at the Word of God, which is sharper than a two-edged sword. Without a heart change, our lives remain like those of the Pharisees, who operated under hypocrisy. Christ continually warned us not to imitate them. Matthew 5:20 says, "For I say to you, that unless your righteousness exceeds the righteousness of the scribes and Pharisees, you will by no means enter the kingdom of heaven."

These self-righteous ones judge people they believe to be worse sinners than themselves. Yet they maintain stiff necks, not willing to yield to the revelation of the truth. However, these people are not easily identified among the saints as they walk like Christians and dress like Christians, and in some cases, look more holy than us with their outward exhibitions of spiritual knowledge and form. We are warned that if our righteousness does not exceed that of the Pharisees, we cannot enter the kingdom of heaven. So as Christians, with our goal to please God and enter into His kingdom, we must search out what exactly is the righteousness of the Pharisees.

The Scribes and the Pharisees seemed to be more concerned with their outward appearance of righteousness as seen by men than the interior condition as seen and judged by God. They did things that would make them look religious and righteous; but their hearts and walk were far from God.

Matthew 23:2–3 says, "The scribes and the Pharisees sit in Moses' seat. Therefore whatever they tell you to observe, that observe and do, but do not do according to their works; for they say, and do not do" (NKJV).

It is a sad situation to know the law and the Word of God but not allow it to bring a change of heart or conviction that leads to repentance and to seek God in order to remove vices and add virtue—like the Pharisees who taught one thing yet did not live it, being hypocrites. Oh how the flesh blinds us in order to stay in control. It doesn't mind us going to church, studying the Word, and even performing good deeds as long as it maintains control and there is no change of heart or action towards seeking God for real change. In fact, the Pharisees of yesterday and today enjoy these religious exhibits, which feed the flesh and the ego but bring no change, as in their own eyes they are righteous and spotless even though in the sight of the Lord their hearts condemn them. The flesh and the carnal life will allow us to live in deception that all is well while our spiritual man starves and dies. The worst thing about the sorry state of living in the flesh is that the more we feed the flesh, the more hardened our hearts become until we are no longer aware that we are walking on the broad way. We have deceived ourselves into thinking we are fulfilling our duties as Christians and that God understands.

The Matter of the Heart

Self-examination is so important. I look at my walk, and there are times when I wonder how I drifted off the path I seemed so comfortable on. Losing focus and becoming mediocre isn't as far removed from us as we may think, especially in a society where there are so many demands for our attention. Our zeal and passion for God seem to wane as we get more familiar with Christianity. The Christian road is a narrow and hard road, and at different times, we lose focus, change priorities, and lose our way. The opposite of pursuit is retreat. In Christian terms, this is backsliding. It is when, instead of pursuing God, we go in the opposite direction and backslide. In most cases, this is a gradual decline, where the believer progressively drifts out of the will and purpose of God.

Throughout this book, we have spoken about pursing God and leaving things behind that hinder and slow down our progress towards intimacy with God. It is very likely that, if you are reading this book, you desire to get closer but also feel far away or that your heart is no longer tender for the things of God. You are not alone in your search. I have felt the same, and there are many others in the same situation. Identifying where we are spiritually is crucial. We need to examine ourselves and our hearts to see whether we are living according to the Word of God and see if there is a change in the passion we once had. If we identify this, we must not explain it away or downplay it. Instead, we must take it to God and return to our first love (Rev. 2:4).

It is essential that we grasp the subtlety and consequences of backsliding. The word used by the prophet Jeremiah in 3:22. Backsliding means turning away from God and worshipping other things. When examining whether we are in a backslidden state, we go straight to the heart of the matter. What is it that we hold dearly in our hearts? There may be everyday things that have replaced the communion and intimacy with God that we once had. We may be too busy; busy doing good and justifiable things. But if these take the place of God, they become idols, and our lives have to be readjusted for us to return to our first love. Revelation 2:4 speaks about leaving one's first love. Continuing in verses 5 and 6, it clearly gives us instructions on how we can restore the broken relationship and reignite the passion we once had. "Remember therefore from where you have fallen; repent and do the first works, or else I will come to you quickly and remove your lampstand from its place—unless you repent" (Rev. 2:5 NKJV).

Remembering from where we have fallen requires us to re-examine ourselves. Second Corinthians 13:5 says, "Examine yourself as to whether you are in the faith. Test yourselves. Do you not know yourselves that Jesus Christ is in you?—unless indeed you are disqualified." When examining ourselves, we must use Scripture and that initial expression of love when we first met God. Has your love gone cold? Did you seek God more diligently in His Word, just to learn about Him and to hear His voice? Did you get so excited about going to church, not just for fellowship but because you were hungry and thirsty for God? Did you share your transformation with the people you met? Did you want to do God's will no matter what the cost? Were you willing to give it your all? If these things were once your desire and they are no longer there, then you must ask yourself, "What has happened to my first love? What has taken its place, and what is the distraction?" Lukewarmness isn't an acceptable fruit of having walked for years with Christ. Yes, many of us will experience it, but we must examine ourselves and then put things in order so that God does not cut us off completely.

Once we have identified the obstacles to this love relationship with God, we must follow the next instruction given in Revelation 2:5–6. We need to repent. To repent means feeling remorseful and sorry and then to change our direction, resolving to live in a manner that glorifies God. Once we have identified areas that we have erred in, our action is to seek God, then once again earnestly seek Him through prayers of repentance and regret.

Dear Lord, I know I've drifted so far away from You, and my life has become so preoccupied with things that don't matter. I'm sorry that I turned my back on You, but my true happiness is with You. Please forgive me for everything I have done that is not according to Your purpose and will for my life. I pray that You will restore the relationship we once had, and I pray for the grace to close every door in my life that will cause me to put you in second place. Lord, have mercy on me, and revive my spirit. In the name of Jesus I pray.

Coming Home

Then He said: "A certain man had two sons. And the younger of them said to his father, 'Father, give me the portion of goods that falls to me.' So he divided to them his livelihood. And not many days after, the younger son gathered all together, journeyed to a far country, and there wasted his possessions with prodigal living. But when he had spent all, there arose a severe famine in that land, and he began to be in want. Then he went and joined himself to a citizen of that country, and he sent him into his fields to feed swine. And he would gladly have filled his stomach with the pods that the swine ate, and no one gave him anything. But when he came to himself, he said, 'How many of my father's hired servants have bread enough and to spare, and I perish with hunger! I will arise and go to my father, and will say to him, "Father, I have sinned against heaven and before you, and I am no longer worthy to be called your son. Make me like one of your hired servants."' And he arose and came to his father. But when he was still a great way off, his father saw him and had compassion, and ran and fell on his neck and kissed him. And the son said to him, 'Father, I have sinned against heaven and in your sight, and am no longer worthy to be called your son.' But the father said to his servants, 'Bring out the best robe and put it on him, and put a ring on his hand and sandals on his feet. And bring the fatted calf here and kill it, and let us eat and be merry; for this my son was dead and is alive again; he was lost and is found.' And they began to be merry. Now his older son was in the field. And as he came and drew near to the house, he heard music and dancing. So he called one of the servants and asked what these things meant. And he said to him, 'Your brother has come, and because he has received him safe and sound, your father has killed the fatted calf.' But he was angry and would not go in. Therefore his father came out and pleaded with him. So he answered and said to his father, 'Lo, these many years I have been serving you; I never transgressed your commandment at any time; and yet you never gave me a young goat, that I might make merry with my friends. But as soon as this son of yours came, who has devoured your livelihood with harlots, you killed the fatted calf for him.' And he said to him, 'Son, you are always with me, and all that I have is yours. It was right that we should make merry and be glad, for your brother was dead and is alive again, and was lost and is found."' (Luke 15:11–32)

Sometimes we allow ourselves to become over committed in many facets of our life. As a result, our time with God gets squeezed, He is no longer our first priority. We need to repent when we get it wrong and even when we regress. We must remember that the prodigal son's father saw him from far off. He was probably looking for him. His heart was yearning in high expectation for the day when he would finally see his son. As he saw him, he ran to him. As God sees us making a step towards Him, we will realise He was right there all the time, just waiting for us to come to our senses. As we draw closer to Him, He will take off the garments of unrighteousness and clothe us with a royal gown. We simply get closer to Him, and God does the transforming work in us.

In the above passage, we see the repentance prayer of the prodigal son. He said, "Father, I have sinned against heaven and in your sight and am no longer worthy to be called your son." He came humbly before his father, broken and contrite and with no pride. Sometimes in order for God to get us back home in His presence, He allows hard times to bring us to our senses—just like the prodigal son. God's Word says that God disciplines those He loves (Heb. 12:6). The prodigal son's father restored him in just the same way God restores us. The son requested to be a servant, but his father accepted him once again as his son. All Christians are required to love those who have fallen away and support them to get back on track and into the love of Christ so as not get themselves entangled with their sin again (James1:23).

Do the First Works

Once we have repented, we also have to change the way we live our lives and live lives that are pleasing to God according to the Scriptures. We need to analyse the things we did in the beginning when we first met God—the things that showed God that we loved Him with everything. Everyone's expression of love will be different. Nevertheless, it touches God's heart.

As we return to re-establish our love relationship with God, we will sometimes find challenging and possibly even hurtful. But we mustn't give up because it hurts or surrender to the pressure to remain without change. When we fall down, we must remember we have a gracious Father who will pick us up. We simply need to seek Him and ask for His help.

Conclusion

We have explored the many obstacles that can get in our way as we pursue God. What we must realise is that God is in pursuit of us. He first loved us and called us to Himself. As we continue in this course of hungering and thirsting after Him, He gives us glimpses of His presence—just enough to keep us thirsting for more. This provides us with the passion and the zeal to overcome every obstacle that comes our way. The Holy Spirit is our guide and coach as we run this race, He will empower us, making us stronger when we feel all has been lost. God is gracious and loving and wants to share this love relationship with us. As we draw near to Him in pursuit, He will draw near to us, transforming us into His image while He uses us to transform the world around us.

When I look at the prodigal son leaving home, I can only imagine that he had a sense of pride, a bounce to his step, money in his pocket, and dreams of making it big. His end was a far cry from this. He came back humbled. Humility was produced through brokenness, and this is what's required for us to recognise God's sovereignty and our inability, as well as our foolishness for believing our strength can achieve anything. We see this same humbling in the life of Nebuchadnezzar (Dan. 4:31–33). He was proud and believed it was his own hands that made him great. God turned him mad, and he lived in a field with animals. It was only through this brokenness and humbling that he was truly able to give glory and honour back to God.

We can get so preoccupied with the rags we are wearing, the external expressions of our disconnection from God, and the evil fruits and behaviours that haunt us. Simply focusing on our externals gives them a greater hold and could distract us from what should be our primary focus of seeking and loving God. The prodigal son ended up living with the pigs, filthy and odorous. We all know what pigs smell like. They love mud. The prodigal son must have looked quite a mess.

For many of us, when we are invited to an event or a dinner, we try our best to be presentable and dress appropriately. Unfortunately, preparing ourselves before we lay at the feet of our Father is a luxury we can't afford. Many times we feel even more disheartened when a sin or habit we want to be free from keeps us enslaved. We must be like the prodigal son and come back to God broken and contrite. We must acknowledge that we cannot meet our needs on our own. Without God we cannot fill the gulf that remains between our lives and God's holy requirement.

As we draw near to God with a humble spirit, seeking restoration, the things that keep us bound will drop off. God will begin to remove the rags in our lives. As the Word says, the light cannot stay where darkness is, and darkness cannot dwell in the same place as the light (John 1:5). So our cure for sin and worldliness is pursuit of Him. As we run toward Him, everything contradictory to light will be eliminated by the light of God. God gives us the grace, and so the sins and behaviours that entangled us will fall away with ease through the power of His Spirit. We mustn't fall into the temptation—one I have on occasion fallen to—of thinking that when God has given us the grace to overcome something, we continue to fall prey to it not because we have an urge to do it but because of the ease with which it dropped away. If we think, *well, this will not hurt,* and take God and His grace for granted, we end up leaving ourselves in a worse state.

God's Word says to draw near to Him and He will draw near to us (James 4:8). As we press into God, we will realise that it is His Will and purpose for us to be clean. As we dwell and grow in intimacy, we begin to look less and less like the world and more and more like Him. What a beautiful thing.

There are many who were once living in the presence of God, in sweet fellowship and communion with Him, who were totally surrendered and sold out for God. Just like the prodigal son, they left with their inheritance and the favour God had bestowed on their lives. This doesn't mean they stopped going to church. Far from this—they had left His heart, and their hearts no longer hungered for Him as before. The joy of knowing God lasted for a season, in the same way as the prodigal's riches, lasted until they ran out through riotous living. We see ourselves facing difficulties and situations that are beyond our own strength and realise that there is something missing. There is a gap, and no human being has the capacity to fill it. We seek others to save us, but this void is created by the absence of our communion with God. Only God can quench our eternal thirst. We seek vices, entertainment, ambition, and engage in carnal activities. Yet after a temporary high, we are left with a hangover from the experience, feeling empty, frustrated, and homesick.

It is in these dark hours and experiences that we attempt to make our way back into His presence. In fact, if things were so jolly and comfortable, some of us would never have taken the first step back into His presence. I thank God for the hard places that have acted as pulling influences, leading me back into His presence and showing me a path through the pain and suffering to where my joy, peace, and love are—in His presence. I thank God for His discipline and pruning because the world has an appeal, and unless God breaks our outer shell with its worldly dependency, we may never grow deeper in the things of God.

Will you stop, pause, and take time out to really evaluate your walk with Him? Will you change things to make love work? He's calling you back to the heart of things. Will you respond? Will you seek Him today? Will you search for Him again just like you would your greatest treasure? Will you put down everything that distracts you from focusing on Him?

He is calling us deeper. He loves us so much and waits around looking at our lives, yearning for us to dwell with Him. He is indeed knocking on the door. Will you let Him in—not just today, but for the rest of your life? Will you give it all for Jesus—not just lip service but by humbling yourself so He can make you whole again as you dwell in His presence? Will you accept His invitation to come away with Him?

This book is a call to all Christians to examine ourselves. We are all at different places, but the challenge is for all of us to come up higher. For those in the pigpen, it is a call to get up and find our way back into the arms of our loving Father—whose arms are ever wide open. For those on the narrow path, it is a call to go deeper in the things of God. Love your weaker brothers and sisters, and support them prayerfully so that they find their way home. For those who are no longer growing spiritually, it is a call to wake up and seek God, and He will open your eyes and ears and remove the spirit of delusion.

In this pursuit of God, making mistakes and falling down is normal. We learn so much through this, which gives us information for the future and enables us to stand firm to finish the race. The problem is the desire to quit when things become hard. The temptation is to discard everything because the process of learning can be challenging and frustrating. As we continue our pursuit of God, remember the words of Paul in 2 Corinthians 4:8–12:

> *We are hard-pressed on every side, yet not crushed; we are perplexed, but not in despair; persecuted, but not forsaken; struck down, but not destroyed—always carrying about in the body the dying of the Lord Jesus, that the life of Jesus also may be manifested in our body. For we who live are always delivered to death for Jesus' sake, that the life of Jesus also may be manifested in our mortal flesh. So then death is working in us, but life in you. (NKJV)*

Can Anything Separate Us from the Love of God?

> *Who shall separate us from the love of Christ? Shall tribulation, or distress, or persecution, or famine, or nakedness, or peril, or sword? As it is written: "For Your sake we are killed all day long; We are accounted as sheep for the slaughter." Yet in all these things we are more than conquerors through Him who*

loved us. For I am persuaded that neither death nor life, nor angels nor principalities nor powers, nor things present nor things to come, nor height nor depth, nor any other created thing, shall be able to separate us from the love of God which is in Christ Jesus our Lord. (Rom. 8:35–39 NKJV)

There is nothing that can separate us from the love of God. God had loved us before we knew Him before we surrendered our lives to Him. He died on the cross with us in mind and with our names written on the palm of His hand. When He went to the cross, He had you in mind. He knew the trials and battles you would encounter along the way when you pursue Him. He knew the besetting sins you would have to lay at His feet as an expression of love. He knew all this, so never run away with the idea that He has left you or forsaken you because of the condition of your soul. No matter where you are at on His narrow path, He is always there watching, waiting, wooing, calling us with compassion, love, and patience. He has loved all of us at our lowest state. I remember Him loving me in bad relationships, bad decisions that took me away from His presence when I was drinking heavily, and yet still the miracles came despite my sin and rebellion. I look back and think about how merciful and gracious God was in loving me, protecting me, talking to me, and fighting for me in the midst of my error.

God simply requires that we do not forget our first love and then settle for second best by receiving the things the world has to offer. God so desires communion, fellowship, and intimacy with us that He sent His Son to the cross to ensure we had a way home and back into His arms. His only request is that we don't sit down, looking at the way home, and then not take it. Oh, how He longs for us; how He wants to make us whole. No matter where you are in your journey, no matter how many valleys you go through and mountains you may have to climb, His love is ever present. His love is always there, never out of reach when we cry, "Abba, Father."

End

Bibliography

Bounds, E M. (2004). *Complete Works of E M Bounds on Prayer, Experience the Wonders of God Through Prayer*. Ada, MI: Baker Books.

Law, W. (2008). *A Serious Call to a Devout and Holy Life*. Newberry, FL: Bridge-Logos Publishing.

Murray, A. (2004). *Absolute Surrender*. North Charleston, SC: Createspace.

Ryle, J. (2014). *Holiness: Its Nature, Hindrances, Difficulties and Roots*. North Charleston, SC: Createspace.

Ryle, J. (2014). *Practical Religion*. North Charleston, SC: Createspace.

Tozer, A. (1948). *The Pursuit of God*. Harrisburg, PA: Christian Publication.

Tozer, A. (1961). *The Knowledge of the Holy*. New York: Harper and Row.

Tozer, A. (1961). *Experiencing the Presence of God*. New York: Random House.

Notes

Coming Soon

AUTHENTIC
Christianity

RUTH CONLON

In *Authentic* author Ruth Conlon explores scriptures that highlight the true marks of authentic Christianity for those in pursuit of a genuine relationship with Christ, while shedding light on dangerous presumptions being made today. In an age where materialism and self-love have taken centre stage, *Authentic* will inspire you to 'deny yourself, carry your cross and follow Jesus'. The book will test your current spiritual condition and challenge readers to grow into maturity and consider what is truly required by sons of God.

Ruth sheds biblical light on topics like holiness, the fruit of the spirit and the wrestle between flesh and spirit that will require readers to make a determined evaluation of the true cost of following Christ. *Authentic* will invite the reader to look closely at their own walk with Christ in light of scripture examining the true condition of the heart. Anyone who honestly desires a genuine relationship with Jesus will be equipped to discern and recognise *Authentic Christianity*.

24242379R00127

Printed in Great Britain
by Amazon